Leading Effective Teams

Essential insights and practical actions
every leader needs to develop and lead
a high performing team

By Martin M Thomas
Edited by Beverley Thomas

*This book is dedicated to
Kate and James,
Kris and Satu,
and David*

www.iwise2.com

About iWise2

iWise2 is a comprehensive on-line leadership and management library and interactive business learning centre.

Our innovative learning materials cover hundreds of leadership and management topics, comprising effective tools to enable you to:

- Build your business leadership and management skills
- Execute and embed effective change
- Improve performance in your team and in your organisation
- Direct your self-development and move ahead in your career

Our members receive access to our full range of learning materials and technical resources, plus interactive training and support through our on-line coaching, forums and more.

Explore now at **www.iWise2.com**

About the Authors

Martin M Thomas, MLM

Martin is a MBA level Director, with over 37 years' experience leading large sales and customer service operations, transformational change, performance improvement and process excellence in the UK and internationally.

Martin's industry experience spans blue-chip organisations in Financial Services, Energy, Commercial Television, Out-sourced Contact Centres, Explosives Fertilisers and Chemicals, and Telecommunications.

His functional responsibilities have included senior Director and General Manager roles in Marketing, Sales, Customer Service, Operations, Change Management, Distribution, IT-Software Development & Networks, Contact Centres, and Service Delivery including accountability for Human Resources and Finance.

Martin is a qualified facilitator and quality trainer who has worked at and with Board level management to drive through cross functional change.

In 2009 Martin was the lead Operations Director implementing the integration of one of the UK's largest financial services mergers.

Martin's extensive knowledge and experience in Change Management, Total Quality Management and Lean Six Sigma has won National Awards, delivered radical performance improvement, including industry leading cost reduction, revenue and profit growth and significant improvements in people engagement.

Martin has a Master's Degree in Leadership and Management (MLM) from Curtin University, Western Australia and an extensive public speaking background.

Martin was an international swimmer for Great Britain, a Commonwealth Games finalist and Civil Service Sportsman of the Year.

Beverley Thomas

Beverley is an experienced Senior Change Leader with over twenty years' experience running major change programmes and projects in blue-chip organisations within the Financial Services, Retail Banking, Insurance, the Oil Industry, Commercial Television, Local Government and the Chemicals Industry in the UK and internationally.

Beverley has successfully led major improvement initiatives from inception to completion (full life cycle) in cultural change, customer service, people management, process improvement, waste elimination and major technology system changes across multiple locations. She has worked with and facilitated board level strategic planning sessions and worked with senior management in developing their Leadership and Capital Stewardship Skills.

Beverley's experience encompasses change and programme delivery under stringent government and industry standards for governance and assurance for the Financial Services, Oil, and Chemical industries and Local Government in the UK and Australia.

Beverley brings collaborative, breakthrough thinking to change management across a wide range of corporate processes and industries. She has delivered programmes as a consultant and a line manager, successfully delivering change in tightly managed, mission critical and complex environments.

Beverley studied Accounting and Corporate Administration at Curtin University in Western Australia.

About this Book

This is a practical book.

It works through 38 characteristics observable in effective teams. To aid focus, these characteristics are grouped into 8 Dimensions that together, present a model of Team Effectiveness.

Designed for the busy leader, each characteristic is brought to life using everyday workplace observations, or insights, together with practical guidance for developing the characteristics of effectiveness in your team.

While the characteristics are grounded in theory and research, the observations and insights come from decades of personal experience leading and managing teams across many industries. These teams cover the full spectrum of team types, team member experience and skill levels, permanent and project, from newly formed to long standing.

The practical guidance offers questionnaires and exercises for self and team assessment. It provides simple processes that you can implement to anchor the characteristics of Team Effectiveness in the way that you and your team work every day. The exercises are not theoretical; they are real workplace procedures. In the main, they come from the real experience and expertise of front line leaders and team members in today's complex, political and rapidly changing organisations.

The guidance also offers suggested applications of structured management tools and techniques. The detailed theory and application of these tools and techniques has not been reproduced in this book, but can be found on our website **www.iwise2.com**.

Being a successful team leader or a member of a highly effective team can be one of the most rewarding times in your career. To create an environment where people can grow, where they can increase and then reach their potential both as individuals and as a team can be extremely fulfilling.

We hope that this book supports you in achieving this aim and we wish you well in your journey as a leader.

Martin M Thomas
Beverley Thomas   iWise2eBusiness Limited June 2011

Contents

Tools, Techniques & Models

The practical guidance in this book suggests the use of various structured tools and techniques to help you develop the characteristics of effective teams. The detailed theory and application of these tools and techniques has not been reproduced here, however, this symbol indicates that you can find detailed explanations and guidance at **www.iwise2.com**.

Introduction

Teams are the building blocks of today's organisations. We are all part of one or more at work every day. Each team is unique. Each team is a distinctive combination of people. Each team has its own individual and diverse challenges.

Today, teams can be a source of strategic competitive advantage and their performance is becoming increasingly important. Having teams is not enough; these teams need to be effective to deliver sustained superior performance.

Moving from a group or a team with average performance to an effective team is not an easy task, nor road to travel.

Like many management concepts, successful teams and teamwork are simple in concept, yet developing them is a highly complex task with many pitfalls.

Our organisations are a complex web of permanent and temporary teams, groups and individuals. We either lead these teams or participate as a member. Our roles vary within them from peer to expert to leader. Membership can fluctuate from permanent to extremely fleeting. The teams themselves can be fixed in organisational structures or positioned to address a specific problem, initiative, programme or project.

Together with these dynamics, different people collaborating in different ways produces endless combinations of personalities, skills, competencies and experience, making each team's structure and performance unique. This uniqueness when combined with the challenges of the task makes running an effective team a challenging responsibility. Making it contribute to superior company performance is a further stretch.

It doesn't matter what teams we are in or whether we lead them or not, we all know that some teams are 'great to be in', some 'good to be in', some are 'OK to be in' and some that are failing, toxic and definitely not 'fun to be a part of'.

Whenever we are in a team that is achieving less than its potential or is frustrating us, we can be puzzled, confused, and even angry at the emotions it stirs in us and the results it achieves or fails to achieve. It can have a dramatic effect on our wellbeing, our morale and our personal effectiveness at work, never mind the organisational consequences of unfocused effort and poor delivery. In many cases the tensions and conflict, atmosphere or relations with the leader can spill over into our home life and in some cases, affect our health.

As a leader of a team we are charged with leading an effective team not an ineffective one. When things go wrong the leader will be accountable. With hindsight, they may look back and wonder 'Could I have done more?', 'Could I have done something differently?' 'Should I have done more to improve the team's effectiveness and help the people reach their potential?'

In summary, teams are important, we are nearly all part of them. They can be great achievers delivering strategic advantage and they can profoundly affect our emotions, self-actualisation and career. As leaders we have prime accountability and responsibility for our teams and their success. Leading effective teams is a critical outcome of our personal leadership.

The impact of teams on business processes, outcomes and individuals in the organisation is what makes teams so important to overall performance.

There seems to be an overt acceptance of the simple concept that a team is a good thing. However there is a '**BUT**'! In our experience over many years, when team members and leaders have been asked to rate the effectiveness of their team, leader and the other teams with whom they interact, low or mediocre scores and perceptions often result. Many are dissatisfied with the way things in the team are working and they feel that they can achieve much more. Many feel dislocated from their organisation, leader or colleagues.

These feelings of dissatisfaction, tension and emotion are heightened during periods of substantial organisational change. For those in 'safe' and key project areas this can result in great opportunities to participate in effective teams and thereby learn and grow. For others, the opposite can occur as jobs are cut, people dislocated, teams merged or broken up and organisational and target operating models reinvented.

These stresses on the individuals within a team can lead to people leaving the organisation and acting as an advocate against people joining the team in the future or simply feeding discontent. Unhealthy team environments can affect the willingness of people to join an organisation as the reputation of what it is actually like to work there can be damaged.

In today's pressured and unstable financial and economic environments, the need to change organisations to be leaner, more focused and more competitive, has never been greater. However at the same time, the demand for increased customer satisfaction and for teams to work well and skilfully together has also never been greater. In times of significant change, it will be the highly effective teams that pull together to deliver results that will significantly contribute to corporate success in the long term.

In spite of this, attaining high performance levels seems elusive for many and gains are hard to hold on to and not easy to define.

It seems that many leaders can 'talk a good game' about having a good team but few seem able to deliver consistently. It is a challenge to deliver and sustain an effective team. There are so many areas that could be improved. Where to start!

That is where this book sets out to help. It provides:

- A definition of Team Effectiveness

- A model of the key Dimensions of Team Effectiveness, outlining areas where a team can focus its attention in order to build, sustain and continually improve effectiveness

- 38 essential characteristics of effective teams, including key insights and practical actions to guide leaders and teams in their development within each Dimension of the model.

The book provides theory, practical guidance, key questions and checklists to help you chart your way to leading or being part of an effective team.

Team Effectiveness

Teams are the basic building blocks of an organisation and we all work within them.

A key element of the performance of the whole organisation is the performance of its teams and the quality of their interactions.

As a result, organisations, leaders and team members are motivated to improve team performance and effectiveness as a source of corporate success, competitive advantage, as well as individual and team growth and development.

But what is 'Team Effectiveness?'

There is no one accepted definition or measurement of team effectiveness.

To deliver Team Effectiveness we must treat it like other aspects of performance. To understand, measure, analyse, improve and recognise it, we need to be able to define it. There is no one accepted definition and many academics point to the difficulty of pinning the concept down. In this book we have defined Team Effectiveness from a practitioner's standpoint, building on the literature and research, primarily using our practical experience.

We start with a basic definition of Team Effectiveness as:

- Satisfying agreed stakeholder requirements

- Engaging everyone in teamwork, learning, developing, growing and improving the individual, processes and the team itself to achieve its potential and its goals

- Having agreed goals, strategies, structure, processes, behaviours, stakeholder support and leadership that enable consistent and improving performance in the above.

This definition grounds Team Effectiveness in the organisational context and the realities of the business needs that surround it. It focuses on people and process development.

This means that Team Effectiveness is about the people in the team, the business around them and their results. Team effectiveness is anchored in delivering results in a balanced way to all stakeholders. It is not an introspective analysis of the innards of a team; rather the team is seen as a vital component of the value chain and a key mechanism for people growth and delivering the organisation's results.

Many academics and writers have studied teams to try and understand how they work and several have proposed models of team performance. One thing is clear from the research: teams that perform do not just happen. Writers have defined factors that influence the effectiveness of teams, ranging from structure to interpersonal team member dynamics, motivation and external influences.

As our definition sees the team in the organisational context, its effectiveness and growth requires sanction from that organisation as well as leadership.

One of the earliest models of Team Effectiveness was by Rubin, Plovnick and Fry[1]. They defined the components of effectiveness as consisting of four layers: Goals, Roles, Processes and Interpersonal Relationships. These were presented in a diagram similar to the triangle used to show Maslow's[2] Hierarchy of Needs.

Katzenbach and Smith[3] see the need for goals, performance, results, personal growth and collective work products as the keys to 'wisdom for teams'. To be fully effective, they specify the importance of appropriate team size, complementary skills, team purpose, team goals, an articulated working approach and a sense of mutual accountability.

Other models like LaFasto and Larson[4] have focused on the need for a 'good' team member, team relationships, problem solving, leadership and the external environment.

Hackman[5] saw a team's effectiveness measured by delivering products and services that exceeded customer expectations, growing team capabilities and satisfying member needs.

Our definition also focuses on meeting agreed customer requirements, whether that customer is internal or external. This means producing outputs and outcomes to a target value with minimum variation. This drives team behaviours to meet defined needs in exactly the same way as Lean and Six Sigma focus on reducing variation in performance around a target value.

This approach to managing variation links to the process improvement concept where over delivery can also be a waste. Delivering above expectations but losing track of costs is not effective.

Our definition extends the definition of customers to all stakeholders including the community. *This later expansion to stakeholders correlates to Schwarz[6] who discusses meeting or exceeding stakeholder standards.*

Hackman[5] sees five necessary conditions for team effectiveness as a team having a team task, clear boundaries, clear authority levels, and membership stability. This is coupled with clear and challenging goals that focus on results. The team requires an enabling structure and norms of conduct to facilitate teamwork. The team also requires a supportive organisation.

Other writers such as Lencioni[7] have focused on what makes teams dysfunctional, citing mistrust, a lack of conflict, commitment, accountability and inattention to results.

A socio-technical view of team effectiveness is the focus of writers such as Cohen, Ledford and Spreitzer[8]. They state that effectiveness comes from the mix of both high performance in terms of an organisation's deliverables and the employee's quality of work life.

The coupling of a team's performance to organisational needs and to a team's rather than an individual's growth, is developed by Tannenbaum, Salas and Cannon-Bowers[9]. They see the logical reason for having a team in the first place, as well as the organisation's support for that team's existence, as critical to ultimate success. Additionally, the team must always understand its changing needs and its resource requirements.

Many other writers have proposed differing components of team effectiveness ranging from styles of decision making, attitudes, and shared concerns through to goal setting and honest communication.

Each piece of research brings its own separate findings, conclusions and perspective. However, regardless of the different sources of the research and propositions, there are some common themes throughout such as goal and role clarity and purpose.

While our view of effectiveness has common grounding in the research and conclusions drawn from a number of academics and writers, it is built from practical experience of running hundreds of teams at all levels within organisations in many different industries.

In this book the key elements underlying the definition and concept of Team Effectiveness are:

- The organisation, as one of the 'stakeholders' in the team supports and sanctions the team's existence

- Understanding when a team is needed or when work should be performed by an individual or group

- The stakeholders and their satisfaction and loyalty are the final arbiters of team performance

- Stakeholder requirements that need to be met are agreed between the team and the stakeholder

- The results needed by the business and its stakeholders drive the team's performance needs

- The results delivered for the stakeholders by the team are objectively measured, not based on opinions

- Clear team identity and purpose

- The team performs effectively and efficiently across its defined and understood value chain

- The team meets its agreed customer requirements first time, every time

- The team delivers its value chain performance and results at the lowest cost without compromising the agreed requirements

- The team engages everyone in the team and aligns their effort and processes to deliver stakeholder requirements

- The team delivers continuous improvement and learning

- The team grows and develops as an entity

- The growth and development of the individuals within the team

- The value chain processes change and improve to meet customer needs and innovation opportunities

- The team has strong management strategies, plans and processes to plan, execute, monitor and learn from performance and activity

- The team has strong situational leadership

- Behaviours that support the development of the team, its individuals, processes and the achievement of its goals

- A commitment to delivery of results and execution of processes

- A clear focus and drive to achieve results

Being effective is critical to the team being a functioning and valued unit within the organisation.

Unfortunately just being effective, although useful and impactful on business performance and stakeholders, is not enough in today's challenging markets and work environments. Effectiveness needs to stand by and include efficiency in order to provide optimum team performance from the perspective of all stakeholders.

It is insufficient to have goal clarity if there is not a consistent drive to improve and make processes more efficient. It is not adequate to have a structure that enables teamwork without recognising that teams are under constant pressure to be efficient and limit cost growth. Having 'adequate' resources is under constant challenge, as more is demanded with less.

The pressures on teams today are substantial and add to the complexity of team management and leadership. Dealing with complexity, ambiguity and enforced change is the norm for many teams within today's organisations. In addition, they have to be nimble and agile to rapidly adapt to changing consumer, market and financial demands.

These organisational realities and constant change make working in teams and sustaining positive morale a challenge for any leader and set of team members.

The other significant change affecting Team Effectiveness is the introduction of technologies, remote working and changing team leadership. Many teams are seeing technologies changing behaviours, whether it changes their prime processes or changes the way they react or communicate. As cost pressures bite and internationalisation grows, teams are required to work together in new ways.

All of these pressures make the need for understanding and delivering Team Effectiveness even more critical than ever before.

Therefore to deliver optimum performance, our definition of Team Effectiveness needs to include:

- Extending the definition of delivery to stakeholders to overtly encompass all activity in the value chain

- Consistency of performance over time

- A strong focus on producing products, services and process activity with minimum variation around target values

- Flexibility, agility and emotional resilience to cope with and implement rapid, radical change and survive upheaval in corporate environments and in stakeholder requirements

This gives a new definition of effectiveness that builds on the foundation definition given at the start of this chapter, using the text added in black below:

An effective team is defined as one that:

1. Satisfies its agreed stakeholder **and value chain** requirements **first time, every time - at lowest cost and with minimum variation**

2. Engages everyone in teamwork, and **continuously** learns, develops, grows and improves the individual, processes and the team itself to achieve its potential and its goals

3. Has agreed goals, strategies, structure, processes, behaviours, stakeholder support and leadership that enable consistent and improving performance in the above

4. **Manages change in an agile, flexible, effective and efficient manner with balanced respect for the needs of the organisation, team and individual.**

The Stakeholders

The definition of Team Effectiveness focuses on the effective and efficient satisfaction of stakeholders needs. The team's stakeholders are:

Customers
Internal and external customers and colleagues that the team delivers products and service to.

Suppliers
Supply products, services and information that enable the team to transform inputs into outputs.

Shareholders
Require the team to effectively and efficiently deliver the organisation's vision, values and mission and meet its financial, governance and risk management requirements.

People
The people within the team and in the wider organisation with whom the team members and the team interact.

Community
The wider external community including regulators, governance bodies, industry and other community groups.

In order to simultaneously meet the requirements of all of its stakeholders, the effective team will need to be aware of and understand each stakeholder need.

The team will then need to balance its efforts to meet each requirement efficiently and effectively.

There will be many requirements, some of which will be ranked by the stakeholder as more important than others. It is vital that the team understands these priorities and how performance and satisfaction will be judged and measured.

These priority needs will form the Critical Success Factors ⌴ for the team.

The Team Effectiveness Model

This book works through 38 characteristics observable in effective teams.

To aid focus, these characteristics are grouped into 8 Dimensions of an integrated, holistic and comprehensive model of Team Effectiveness.

Use the model in different ways that suit your needs as a:

- *high level guiding framework and road map to help you assess your team's effectiveness*

- *checklist where you can scan over the various topics and ascertain your strengths and weaknesses*

- *systematic approach that walks you through the building blocks of a successful team.*

The Model

The model sets out 8 Dimensions that summarise the 38 essential characteristics of effective teams.

The definition of Team Effectiveness

An effective team is defined as one that:

1. Satisfies its agreed stakeholder and value chain requirements first time, every time - at lowest cost and with minimum variation

2. Engages everyone in teamwork, and continuously learns, develops, grows and improves the individual, processes and the team itself to achieve its potential and its goals

3. Has agreed goals, strategies, structure, processes, behaviours, stakeholder support and leadership that enable consistent and improving performance in the above

4. Manages change in an agile, flexible, effective and efficient manner with balanced respect for the needs of the organisation, team and individual.

The core principles

At the heart of the model are two core balancing principles that are both needed across all of the activity of a team and all of the Dimensions. The concept is that these two principles need to be in harmony for a team to be effective in today's business environment:

Being effective
Doing the right things

Being efficient
Doing things right

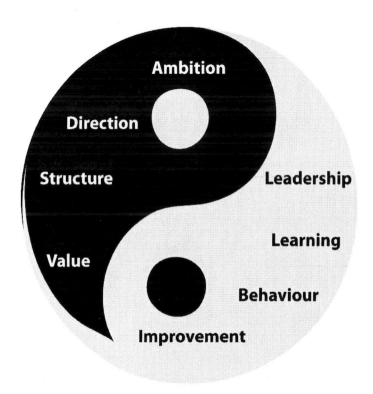

The two principles balance each other. As in the Ying and Yang philosophical model that uses balance as its theme, each principle shows a dot of the other colour – the other principle. This indicates that everything in Team Effectiveness, like the philosophy's view of life, is not black and white. There are elements of each embedded in the other.

This presents a strong philosophical and practical basis for the model, that is, for shareholders' needs to be delivered in a manner that balances effectiveness and efficiency. These principles work in tandem and need to balance each other for Team Effectiveness to be achieved.

At times one side will dominate the other but balance is important over the long term for sustainability. Too much focus on efficiency will eventually erode effective delivery and the stakeholder need will be under threat of compromise or failure in delivery. Too much focus on effectiveness can mean meeting the need at any cost, leading to financial failure, excess and waste – waste, which at some time will need to be eliminated, potentially at great cost.

When using the model, these core principles should be viewed as:

Balanced effective and efficient delivery of the results defined by the stakeholders

This underpins the way in which all activity should be conducted to achieve the end results. It reinforces the first part of our definition of Team Effectiveness:

Satisfies its agreed stakeholder and value chain requirements first time, every time - at lowest cost and with minimum variation

The Dimensions

The model has 8 Dimensions. The Dimensions provide areas of focus for a leader or a key team member to consider when working to improve Team Effectiveness.

The first four of the Dimensions have a bias towards effectiveness and establishing the right thing to do, and the right way to do it. These are the:

- **Ambition,** knowledge and commitment needed to be an effective team in the first place.

- **Direction** set by locking in the goals and aligning them to stakeholder needs.

- **Structure** required for the optimal deployment of resources.

- **Value** added by delivering superior performance across the value chain to meet stakeholder needs.

The other four Dimensions have a bias towards efficiency, delivering and improving the right things. They focus on behaviour and actions.

- **Improvement** is a strong focus and is continuous across processes, the team and individuals.

- **Behavioural** norms that enable success across all aspects of performance.

- **Learning** is required to facilitate growth and development across the processes, team and individual needs.

- **Leadership** is required to coach the team and lead the management of change and agility, to meet new demands.

Effectiveness and efficiency are required in balance across all 8 Dimensions.

1 Ambition

Knowing when a team is needed, and that it is a team that you want to lead is the first step on the journey.

From here you can take action to develop teamwork, build relationships and set a plan for the team's development. With the commitment of your team to this development path, together, you are on your way towards becoming the effective team.

Effective Team Characteristic 1:
Knows what a team is, why and when it is needed

Not all deliverables, tasks or projects require a team. Many tasks and projects can be delivered more effectively without the use of a team, either by a group, or an individual.

As a leader, it is critical that you can evaluate and implement an operational structure that is able to deliver the organisation's objectives with your resources.

Knowing when teams and sub-teams are needed, as opposed to groups and individuals, is the first step in the optimal deployment of different combinations of resources.

Knowing that you want a team in the first place, and why, needs to be your first consideration when planning any team building or development activity. Applying team building and development principles and techniques to a group who do not need and do not use a 'team dynamic' can be a poor use of time, energy and money.

Equally, trying to force-fit a group or set of individuals into a team structure when one is not required will not be productive and will frustrate the individuals concerned.

As a leader wanting to develop an effective team, you need to start by looking at your area of responsibility and identify why the collection of people you lead needs to be a team.

Leader Exercise: Do you need a team?

Examine your direct reports and list why it is important for this collection of people to be a team.

Team Exercise: Why are we a team?

As a team list why it is important for you to be a team.

Effective business units are made up of a complex combination of individuals, groups and teams.

Your 'team' may in fact be a group or a collection of sub-teams who work relatively independently and therefore have different leadership needs. To be effective as a leader you need to use the right leadership approach for the different teams, sub-teams, groups and individuals that you manage.

Individuals are of course easy to identify. But how do you spot the difference between a group and a team?

Spot a Group

A group within the workplace can be defined as:

A collection or network of people that are considered to be related and interact in some way, know of each other's existence, share some characteristics and perform some related tasks to achieve particular objectives.

A simple example would be where the people who report directly to you all have separate objectives or customers and do not work together to achieve their objectives or to satisfy their customers. They are related in that they work for you and in a common function or line of business.

Another common example is a Board of Directors. They are clearly related to the company they serve; they share similar characteristics and perform interrelated tasks that assist the company deliver to its shareholders. They will exhibit some but not all of the characteristics required to be defined as a team.

One useful way that people combine at work to achieve certain objectives is to form a group. These groups can be formal or informal and can often be large in size with membership selected by role, loose affiliation or general interest.

Spot a Team

Defining a team could be a book on its own! Some characteristics that help differentiate a team from a group include:

- Common purpose and goals
- Common norms of behaviour with strong inter team member trust and 'gel'
- Interdependence in delivering results
- A mutual sense of accountability and responsibility
- A collaborative, cohesive way of using resources and sharing expertise
- Shared processes, principles and working practices
- Commitment to development and improvement as a unit
- Combining skills to achieve results that are greater than what could be achieved from one individual - synergy
- A combined sense of achievement and fun
- Setting and rising to demanding challenges together
- Questioning team performance and conducting self-analysis
- Learning together
- Shared leadership
- Usually compact in size between 4 and 12 people
- Members are selected with intent and due process

Teams can be defined as:

a collection of people that exhibit all the characteristics of a group with the addition of:

shared agreed goals, development of their own processes, a commitment to learn, mature and improve as a unit. They have team feelings, trust and emotions and need to build, grow and develop as a unit. They recognise that their results and their own success and the success of others are intrinsically interdependent.

As you can see, a team is not a group with a nice label 'team' added. It has a different dynamic to a group. Teams are needed when *interdependent effort and teamwork* is the best way to achieve an objective.

However, for interdependent effort to actually be *effective* as a means of achieving your objectives, you will need to ensure that your team has the characteristics of effective teams.

What are you leading or a member of?

Teams and groups are different and require different leadership. As a leader, it is important to know what you are leading or as a member of a team or group, you need to know the expectations of behaviour and performance of each.

When you assess your team's structure and the way that tasks are actually performed, it may be evident that in reality there are a number of sub-teams and or groups within the primary team identity.

There may also be groups and teams outside your own team that individuals in your team also belong to or are involved in.

While these affiliations may either be formal and visible on the organisation's structure chart, or informal, they will still be a known and effective means of getting things done.

At best, these informal groupings can be made up of colleagues who transcend formal structures to rally together to 'get things done', at worst, they can form self-serving or destructive factions or 'clubs' that create blockages in the organisation.

The different needs of these entities increase the complexity of the people, processes and interactions you lead and manage.

Knowing what teams and groups exist inside or touch your area of responsibility gives you great insight into decision-making and power, as well as the location and structure of expertise and peer support.

Examining the formal and informal groupings in the context of your objectives and workflows is important. This will help you understand whether you have the most effective structure to enable you to successfully deliver the needs of your stakeholders.

Once you are satisfied that you have the most effective configuration of groups and teams, tailor your leadership, resourcing and development activity to the different needs of each unit.

Leader Exercise: Assess your structure

List the primary teams, sub-teams and groups, formal and informal inside your area of responsibility. List the groups and teams that your team members additionally belong to. You could also add groups and teams that touch your leadership area where they have the potential to significantly impact your performance.

My direct leadership has the following:

Groups:

Teams:

My team members including myself are part of the following:

Groups:

Teams:

Map these teams and groups onto a Relationship Diagram. Review your diagram against your formal organisation chart and against key processes and workflows.

Ask yourself:

■ How accurately does the current organisation chart represent how things really get done?

■ Would you make any changes?

■ Do you have teams in all areas where you need teams?

■ Is planned team building and development activity focused on them?

Effectiveness Tips:

✓ Know the difference between a team and a group

✓ Know when tasks, processes and deliverables require a team, rather than a group or individual

✓ Identify the teams and groups that exist in your area of responsibility

✓ Ensure that your structure of teams, groups and individuals is effective in terms of achieving your deliverables

✓ Focus team building and development activity on teams

Effective Team Characteristic 2:
Knows what teamwork is and then develops it

Teamwork is easy to say. When we have a team, we generally expect 'teamwork' to be the means by which things get done. However, anyone with experience leading or working in a team will know that in reality, teamwork usually doesn't just happen on its own. It needs deliberate cultivation – which is why many leaders are keen on team building, 'away days' and other offsite and social events, as a means of instilling or improving teamwork.

The definition of teamwork may seem obvious on the surface, even glib. However, if you asked your team to define teamwork and how they could specifically use it to increase their effectiveness both as individuals and as a team, you might be surprised at the range of responses. Working through such a range of views as a team and trying to form a consensus would be a useful start to raising awareness and further developing teamwork in your team.

Team Exercise: Improving teamwork

Discuss the following as a team or in small groups. Record all responses and work through them together to see what insights result. Take joint ownership of any actions that you might agree.

What is teamwork?

- Of the teams that your team members are involved in, or interact with, which exhibit teamwork?

- Rank these teams' teamwork from best to worst

- Explain the rationale for your rankings

- What are the key characteristics that separate the best from the worst?

- What are the key learnings from this?

How can we improve our teamwork?

- In which of our processes and procedures could we use teamwork to improve our effectiveness?

- Specifically, what would this look like in each process and procedure? What impact would this have on our results?

- Are there any barriers to good teamwork, either in this team or in the wider organisation?

- What actions can we take to remove these?

- For this team, what is our common expectation of 'behaviours' that facilitate teamwork?

- What are our sanctions when these behaviours are not present?

- Are there any teamwork issues that impact our interactions with other teams and processes in the organisation?

- How can we address these?

One way of assessing whether your team exhibits teamwork is to use the '11Cs of Teamwork' as a framework to start a discussion before drilling down into specifics for a deeper understanding.

The 11Cs of Teamwork:

1. **Commitment**: Members and the team as a whole commit and promise to deliver agreed outputs, outcomes and behaviours

2. **Cohesion**: The team members gel and show unity of purpose and action

3. **Collaboration**: The team members join forces with each other to achieve a specific goal

4. **Consistency**: The team and its members are dependable and deliver what is expected all the time

5. **Communication**: The team communicates in all directions inside and outside the team effectively

6. **Coordination**: The team allocates resources, time and effort in a way that meets the task, team and individuals' needs in an optimum manner

7. **Contribution**: The team members improve, augment and participate in team processes

8. **Cooperation**: Team members encourage and assist other team members and processes

9. **Collective**: Team members see the team as an entity with a common purpose and goals

10. **Conflict**: The team has a healthy level of conflict focused on improving results, using critique not criticism

11. **Challenging**: The team challenges the status quo and seeks improvement in processes and outcomes for all stakeholders in a balanced manner

Remember, being in a team is not the same as being a team, or working as a team.

Effectiveness Tips:

✓ Gain consensus in your team as to what teamwork means – use the 11C's as guidelines

✓ As a team, agree what behaviours and ways of working are expected to be observed in order to support teamwork

✓ Agree processes for dealing with each other when teamwork across the 11Cs is not evident

Effective Team Characteristic 3:
Knows the type of team they are, and its development needs

The type of team that you have will determine how it is led, managed, structured and developed. Understanding the type of team that you have is key to enabling you to structure your resources most effectively and tailor team building and development activity to the specific needs of your team.

There are a number of models of team types.

Hackman[5] described four types of team ranging from 'Manager Led' to 'Self-Governing'. These are useful descriptions, each brings advantages and disadvantages and they have different development needs. The categories below are adapted from Hackman:

Manager Led
Manager controls the processes and goals of the unit, determines its structure and performance needs, as well as relationships within and external to the team.

Self-Managed Teams
As above, but the process is managed by the team members.

Self-Designing Teams
As above, except the team sets its own performance targets. Managers facilitate the provision of resources and manage important extra-team relationships.

Self-Governing Teams
As above, except the team takes responsibility for determining the rationale for what is done as well as what is actually done.

The teams and sub-teams you lead or are a part of, may comprise different types such as those outlined above.

Clearly as a leader, the style and actions you adopt will be different for each type of team. If you have many sub-teams that are different, you will need to be able to flex your leadership style according to their differing needs.

Leader Exercise: Team types, using Hackman[5] as a guide

- What are the team types for each of the teams you identified earlier in 'Assess your structure'?

- What does your answer imply for the leadership and management approaches you might take?

- What does your answer imply for the development needs of the teams?

- What does this imply for the development approaches you might take and for the team's development path?

- How could you improve your approach to leading these teams from what you have reviewed above?

- How would you measure any improvement?

Ratcliff et al[10] had another view of team types, ranging from 'Simple' to 'Problem Solving' and the implication of each for ideal team sizes. This view of team types focuses on the way work flows in the team, and its challenges.

Type	Volume of transactions/load	Team size
Simple Team	Large volumes of basically the same tasks	Size based on volume, time and a person's capacity to handle the load per unit of time
Relay Team	Item passed from one person to another in a specified sequence in order for tasks to be performed on the object at each step	Size based on cycle time required for the process and the complexities of each task with the smooth flow of work and no rework
Integrative Work Team	Simultaneous tasks performed on service or product at the same time that are related to each other	Size based on task time and the specialisation of tasks involved in completing the cycle time required to complete the process
Problem Solving Team	Combines competencies and experience to tackle more ambiguous tasks and challenges	Size based on the complexity of the problem, the time frame required, the importance and urgency of the challenge and the level of interaction needed

Leader Exercise: Team types using Ratcliff[10] et al as a guide

Again, consider your teams from the previous exercises.

- What do these team types suggest about the types of teams you manage or lead?

- What do these team types suggest about the size of your team? Are your teams sized effectively?

- What are the implications for your leadership of these different types of team?

- How should you structure and manage your resources? Are the volume and cycle time measures and associated processes clearly understood, enabling the right type of team to be deployed?

- What are the implications for team building or team development activities?

These different team types give you an insight into different ways of looking at teams and that different leadership and development approaches are required to achieve effective performance.

Effectiveness Tip:
✓ Understand the type of team you are managing, tailor your leadership style, resourcing and team development accordingly

Effective Team Characteristic 4:
Balances task, team and individual needs

As a leader, a critical element of your role is orchestrating the delivery of the tasks that you are accountable for, through the efforts of your team while simultaneously ensuring that the needs of your team and of each individual within it are also met.

Effective teams deliver results. The needs of the team and of each individual are not sacrificed in order to achieve this. The needs of all three are kept in balance.

The needs of the task are essentially its completion, at the required level of quality, within the required timeframe.

The needs of the individual are by definition, individual. They may include: a need to work on tasks that suit his or her interests, experience and abilities, a need to be challenged, a need to be given every chance to succeed, a need to receive recognition and opportunities to develop and to progress.

The needs of the team are to be built, maintained and developed in order to enable a high level of performance.

You can imagine that from time to time, these needs may conflict. For example, a lengthy, tedious task may conflict with an individual's need to be challenged and to do interesting work that will create opportunities for career progression. A task with a seemingly impossible deadline may conflict with a team's need to be seen as successful and high performing. An individual's need not to work on the weekend for family reasons, may conflict with the team's need to have everyone contribute in order to meet an important deadline.

As a leader, you need to maintain an awareness of all these needs and manage any factors within your control to prevent them from conflicting. Where a factor outside your control creates such a conflict, you need to use your skills to mitigate as much as possible, the impact of the 'unmet' need on the relevant party.

John Adair's[11] model of Action Centred Leadership (ACL) is a very useful and simple model used to illustrate the interaction of task, team and individual needs.

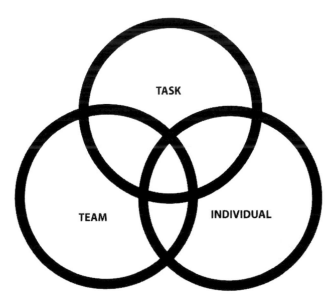

Figure 1 Action Centred Leadership: Interaction of Needs

The forces that pull the circles away from each other may be strong. As a leader your task is to mitigate these divisions and work to create stronger forces that pull the circles together and maintain the balance.

Leader Exercise: Balancing task, team and individual needs

Examine your team.

- Where is the balance of focus and effectiveness? Is it in the task, the team or the individual?

- What can you observe that supports your view?

- What is driving you to allocate your leadership time and effort in this way? What are the implications of this?

- List the forces that are acting on the task, the team and individual needs (i.e. the forces that are enabling or preventing them from being met).

- How would you summarise any imbalance? What needs to change?

Effectiveness Tips:

✓ Use the Action Centred Leadership (ACL) model[11] and its three interlocking circles to identify where the needs of the task, the team and the individual intersect or standalone

✓ Balance the needs of tasks, team and individuals. Be alert to any significant conflicts between them

✓ Manage any significant conflicts – resolve them if this is possible, mitigate the impact if it is not

Effective Team Characteristic 5: Develops individuals

Effective teams need effective individuals. As a leader, when you act to build teamwork and develop your team, you will also need to consider the development needs of each individual. A more developed individual brings a more positive influence to the team dynamic and greater competency to add to the overall level of team competency.

Individuals with unmet development needs can impair the team's effectiveness, as their competence and perhaps motivation levels will not be as high as they could be.

Individuals need objectives, goals, clear measures of performance and action plans as much as teams. In particular, they need to be able to cascade these to the teams they lead and participate in elsewhere in the organisation.

Measuring an individual's performance and progress begins with goal setting. Ensure that each individual's goals are aligned to the goals of the team. Each individual should understand the needs of the team and the part their personal contribution plays in the delivery of the overall team goals.

Individuals also need regular one on one time with their line manager in order to raise issues, understand and measure their progress and discuss any emerging development needs on a timely basis. When used effectively, these sessions can be a very powerful tool to facilitate a team member's professional development.

Record your discussions so that you can build on them and review progress. Ensure that any development plans and actions that are agreed are implemented.

These meetings should focus on the individual's development needs. It is useful to discuss these needs in the context of the team's development as a whole.

Unfortunately, too often, these meetings are the first to be deferred or cancelled at busy times or when more pressing business issues arise. Although there are times when this can't be avoided there are some simple strategies that you can employ to help, for example:

- Commit in your objectives to holding a set number of one to one meetings with each of your direct reports during the year. Ensure that they do the same with their direct reports.

- Put these meetings in your diary for the next 12 months now, so that you don't need to find a way to fit them into your schedule later - when it's full.

- As a team, reinforce that one to ones are essential to the team's performance management and development culture. Set an expectation as a team that these meeting will take place.

- Publicly state to your team that it is not acceptable for you to defer or cancel their one to one's. Commit to re-instating, within a set time frame, any that really need to be moved.

As well as allocating the appropriate amount of time for these discussions, consideration also needs to be given to the format and to the environment. The environment needs to be 'safe' enough to allow both parties to be open and to raise and talk through issues as honestly as they can.

As an example, it is common to see one to one meetings being held over coffee. This may be right for some, with the less formal environment encouraging deeper, more open and honest communication.

However, others (and in certain situations) may not feel that appropriate seriousness is being given to the occasion. Always check that your colleague who reports to you is comfortable with the proposed length of time, format and the environment for the discussion. Don't assume that what works for you, also puts them at ease.

While taking care to individualise these meetings, you will also need to take care not to be seen to favour one person over another. If one person always gets taken for coffee and others do not, be aware of how this might be seen and the potential impact on reputation and culture. Check the perception of fairness and professionalism against the casual atmosphere that results. Does this fit with the organisation's culture as well as the needs and expectations of the individual?

It is worth noting that these one to one meetings do not replace the need for regular communication and the casual conversations that 'oil' the flow of the work machine day to day and that build relationships and understanding.

Another approach to individual, as well as team development is coaching. For example, external coaches from outside the line management or outside of the organisation can be very effective. External coaches rarely have the opportunity to observe the coachee in their normal working environment. Special care is therefore needed to ensure that these sessions have the right focus on the individual's specific development needs. The structure of the coaching sessions and the involvement of the line manager also need to be taken into account and clearly defined.

✓ Effective teams need effective individuals. Prioritise both individual and team development

Effectiveness Team Characteristic 6:
Knows the difference between team building and team development – and when to use them

The terms 'team building' and 'team development' are commonly used interchangeably, when in fact, they are two distinct activities, with separate objectives and processes.

Team Building

Team building is exactly that - building the team. It is about bringing together individuals and groups who did not choose each other, to form a cohesive and collaborative unit. This aims to improve the performance of the individuals and the team as a whole.

Team building activities see the team as an entity. They aim to improve the team's internal workings by forging strong working relationships between the team members.

Often, team building exercises have nothing to do with usual work tasks, but tend to be abstract exercises and events that develop problem solving skills and cooperation. We have all heard of or some may even have been on, the proverbial 'raft building' exercise. Activities of this nature are designed to take team members away from the usual working environment and give them unrelated tasks that help the team focus solely on coming together and learning more about each other.

Team building is particularly needed when there is a change in the team membership or when there are significant performance or working relationship issues. It should also be used regularly during the life of a team.

Team development

Team development has a different focus to team building.

Team development facilitates the process of continuous improvement in a team's performance. It is often supplemented by team building.

While team building focuses on relationships, team development focuses on a team's tasks and objectives and aims to improve how effectively and efficiently these can be delivered.

Team development views the team in its organisational context. It therefore considers the internal needs of the team as well as its interactions and its position in the wider organisation.

Team development is a long-term commitment, but is not something that sits on the shelf only to be revisited sporadically or when performance issues arise. It is a critical facilitator of continuous performance improvement and therefore needs to be permanently on the team's agenda. The effective team uses systems and processes to maintain a focus on team development.

Team development defines the team's performance measures and impacts the perceptions of stakeholders. Team development also captures how the team members view their own performance and how they feel about it.

Team development focuses on continually improving teamwork within the team and between the team and other parts of the organisation. This activity will give way to team building when there is a very specific need to inject a focused effort on team relationships.

Team development is a long term approach that addresses both real and perceived problems in the team's performance. It always has an improvement focus.

Leader Exercise: Team development

Look at the year ahead and assess what team development activity needs to take place. Plan it in. Discuss with the team the objectives and the scope of the required development activity and decide on the best format to achieve these objectives.

Team development activity could include for example, the team rating itself against each of the characteristics of the effective team set out in this book. There are a number of assessment tools available to help you assess your current effectiveness and identify development opportunities, such as the Team Effectiveness Model Assessment Tool™ (TEMAT™), available for download at **www.iwise2.com**.

Using the results of your assessment, agree as a team any actions that need to be taken to improve performance. Review your progress through the year.

Recognise the mix of team building and team development your team requires. Holding just another 'raft building' event for the fun of it is lazy and will probably waste an opportunity to really move the team towards its development objectives. Each activity (that you spend your organisation's time and money on!) should have a clear, documented objective and purpose, specific to the development needs of your team, its personalities and its people.

Take care when choosing team building activities – they should be enjoyable and engage everyone.

When should you use team building and when should you use team development?

Team building tends to come in at specific times in short sharp bursts to strengthen working relationships, fix issues and anything that is 'off balance' within the team. The need for team building can be urgent and it can be delivered in the short term. You can use the Urgent-Important Grid[14] 📖 (see page 90) to help you prioritise team building needs. Team building can improve performance by focusing on the interactions, networking and support required for the team members.

Team development on the other hand, looks at the team's process for continuous improvement and making the most of opportunities over the longer term. The rewards are bigger, but they take longer to realise. As such, some team leaders might be tempted to just focus on team building as a proxy for team development. That is too easy. Team development focuses on opportunities to grow and the continuous improvement of processes, technologies, people and their interrelationships. Great leaders do not shy away from such an opportunity to work at this deeper level with their team over a sustained period of time.

Effective teams undertake both team building and team development during their lifespan. They are able to identify issues as they grow and use team building to address problems and new challenges, such as changes in the team's structure or composition.

It is important to remember that a team's dynamics changes every time someone joins or leaves the team. A new team is formed every time this happens. New skills, experiences, ideas, behaviours, passions and competencies are added to the team, or taken away with every change. This can cause subtle or not so subtle shifts in the team's culture.

Consider the possible need to undertake new team building or development activity when this happens.

Changes in the environment can also change the team dynamic, such as a reorganisation of the company, or a related unit, or of suppliers or processes. Effective teams are aware of the potential impact of such changes on them and their performance and will restructure or adapt their activities accordingly. This in turn may result in a new team and new development needs. Maintain awareness of any such changes and openly discuss their potential impact in the context of the team's needs, performance and development objectives.

Team development and team building cannot be left to chance. They require leadership skills, focus, specific development competencies and attention. They also require planning and measuring as a key business activity as part of your goals, objectives, plans, budgets and performance management processes.

Effectiveness Tips:

✓ Understand the difference between team building and team development – and when to use them

✓ Understand when you are team building

✓ Understand when you are undertaking team development

✓ Monitor changes in the team and in the organisation that result in the need for either team building or team development

✓ Understand your team building and development requirements and plan these activities to meet specific objectives

✓ As a leader, assess your team development capability. Use external expertise or other training to improve your skills

✓ Document and regularly review the team building and development plan

✓ Use feedback from the team to improve team building and development activities

✓ Measure team members' satisfaction with the amount and quality of the team building and development they undertake

✓ Correlate the satisfaction measures with other key performance indicators to ensure the development activity is effectively improving in overall performance

Effective Team Characteristic 7:
Knows where it is on the development path

Teams go through stages of development. They move around these stages as their challenges, structure and membership changes.

The well-known stages of a group's development derived from Tuckman's[12] model are:

Forming
The tentative unclear phase characterised by a degree of anxiety and impression building.

Storming
The group is in conflict with some identity beginning to emerge

Norming
Identity stronger with increased internal understanding.

Performing
Strong focus on performance with established relationships within the team.

Dorming
Team is complacent and does not challenge itself. Self-protectionism is at work as is rejection of anything that challenges the cultural fit.

Adjourning
The closure, disbanding or parking of a team.

Teams will move through these stages, but may not necessarily improve their effectiveness as they go.

Indeed, groups can sometimes be more effective in the Storming phase when they are willing to challenge assumptions and the status quo.

Teams can equally move backwards through the stages. While these stages are not an exact science, they are a useful guide.

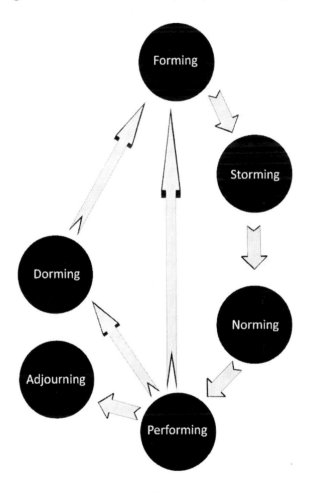

Figure 2 Adapted from Tuckman's[12] The Forming, Storming, Norming, Performing, Dorming and Adjourning model

---

Team Exercise: Tuckman's Team Stages

Together with your team, use Tuckman's model of team stages to discuss:

- where each member sees the team in that development cycle and why

- the key characteristics of your team and how they map to the characteristics of Tuckman's team stages?

- what can be expected from the team as it progresses through each stage and how the team will recognise the behaviours and the developments

- negative characteristics that may arise in the later stages, such as, a lack of healthy challenge, complacency, Groupthink and the team resting on its laurels

---

In addition to Tuckman's[12] model, the 'High Performance Curve' can also be very powerful as a basis for discussing the team's development path.

The High Performance Curve

The High Performance Curve defined by Jon Katzenbach and Douglas Smith[3] presents a model of a team's growth in relation to the needs of the business and of the team members.

The model suggests that businesses are formed of groups and various types of team, defined by the needs of the business and the level of team effectiveness the people are willing to deliver together.

In the organisation, groups and teams will be at different stages of development along the High Performance Curve. Each will have a different impact on business performance and will work together and interact with the business, suppliers and the external environment in different ways.

The curve presents the ultimate in team performance as the High Performing Team.

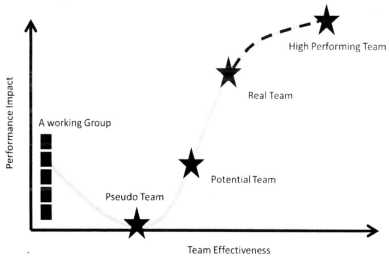

Figure 3 The High Performance Curve: team growth path

Working Groups

In the model, Working Groups are a loose association of individuals. The people in the group mainly work separately; they do not come together and combine with the other members - they work alongside them. Working Groups are needed when there is a need for cooperation between people but little need for close bonds across all the members as a whole. Groups can have varying impact on business performance depending on the seniority and expertise of the members. They often form to address governance and control needs and to share information.

Pseudo-Teams

In Pseudo-Teams, friendships are developed and people work closely together. The people are very supportive of each other and the team members value the relationships between them. Team members are keen to complete tasks but can prioritise friendships and working relationships above this. Team members are anxious about conflict and avoid it wherever possible. They work hard to protect the relationships often at the expense of task completion. Team Effectiveness is much higher than in a Working Group. The team feels that it is a strong team because of the close friendships formed, and as a result, views itself as delivering a strong business benefit. The business impact can be positive, reflecting a degree of teamwork and team effectiveness. However the imbalance in perspectives and priorities (team and relationships versus goals, business and stakeholder needs) means that the Pseudo-Team's impact against all stakeholder requirements is less than optimal.

Potential Teams

A Potential Team results when the business has a strong need for a team but Team Effectiveness is poor. The people exist in a defined and identifiable structure that is either temporary or permanent. They are working together and have a balanced perspective on the needs of the business, the team and the individual. They are a Potential Team as they have developed the basic framework for a Real Team but are not delivering on the requirements consistently. The team is typified by internal conflicts, communication misunderstandings and decisions that are not enacted by all or poorly executed.

Internal relationships can be strained and individuals can find themselves isolated. Factions develop but are broken down by the team as it attempts to improve. The team lurches more than flows from task to task and issue to issue. Teamwork is evident but is inconsistent.

While Team Effectiveness is greater than that of a Pseudo-Team, it has not reached its full potential. Business impact is improved, but is far from what can ultimately be delivered.

Real Teams

Real Teams mature from Potential Teams. They increase their effectiveness and make a bigger impact on business performance and stakeholder satisfaction. The team forms into an entity with strong teamwork. They are focused on business goals and objectives, support each other and ensure that individual development is appropriate. The needs of the task, team and individual are well balanced. They have developed strong processes for communication and decision making, and have a culture that improves team performance.

High-Performing Teams

High-Performing Teams mature from Real Teams. They develop effective performance across the whole range of stakeholder needs. They are efficient in their delivery and have a strong identity. They make and keep commitments and provide strong mutual support. Recognition and celebration of success is appropriate and enhances performance. They are recognised by their stakeholders as high performing. They deliver strong business performance and impact, balanced by the growth and development of the team and the individuals. They deliver more than a Real Team in consistency and use conflict, self-assessment and learning to improve performance for stakeholders.

They consistently deliver a high level of Team Effectiveness.

This model can stimulate a very interesting team debate as to what it means to be at each stage and what behaviours may be demonstrated by individuals and by the team at each stage.

It also brings into focus Pseudo-Teams, which are really groups forming into teams or teams disintegrating or showing no characteristics of teamwork. These are often identified by team members themselves as well as others, and are typified by the feeling that they are a 'team' on the organisation chart in name only.

It also brings into focus the challenges facing the team to become a 'Real Team', what actions the team needs to take and what behaviours it needs to adopt to move up the curve to be a 'High-Performing Team'.

Team Exercise: The High Performance Curve

Use the High Performance Curve and the definitions of each team type to stimulate debate in your team as to where your team is on the curve and where it would like to be.

As a team, agree what actions you will commit to in order to effect this change, and how you will monitor your progress.

Effectiveness Tips:

✓ Know the stages of team development that your team will progress through on its way to becoming an effective team

✓ Assess where you are on the development path and the actions that you need to take to progress to each stage

✓ Feed these actions into your team development plan

Effective Team Characteristic 8:
Knows why teams fail

While teams have enormous potential to be successful, achieve, grow and develop, they can also fail. Understanding the reasons why teams fail can act as an early warning mechanism for potential problems, enabling swift or preventative action. They can also act as a checklist of actions to assist a team's progress towards effectiveness.

Here are some of the key reasons why teams fail:

1. Purpose not clear
2. Goals and objectives not clear or realistic
3. Roles, accountabilities and responsibilities not clear
4. Norms and behaviours ill defined
5. Customers, suppliers and stakeholders not supportive
6. Leadership ineffective
7. Empowerment and engagement weak
8. Conflict management poor
9. Lack of adequate planning and review
10. Lack of training and education
11. No common purpose
12. Resources ineffectively used
13. Lack of honest and open communication
14. Failure to use expertise and experience
15. Inability to change or adapt to new challenges
16. Destructive behaviours
17. Lack of resilience and staying the course

One particular source of failure that is not always obvious is how well equipped team members are for working in a team.

As organisations tend to base their reward systems on individual performance (and this is important to most), people may be used to working and being rewarded as individuals. Yet, many requirements of an organisation can only be accomplished through people working together. This need is being amplified by increasing change and complexity. It can therefore be argued that the strength of an organisation depends on how effectively individual talent combines to deliver team results.

It is important to understand that when teams form or individuals join who are used to working independently, there can be a gap in the attitudes, skills and knowledge necessary to participate in and contribute fully to a team. This can be a significant blockage to a team's effectiveness and success. This is when team building and team development are critical.

As a leader, be aware of this dynamic as it can be a key reason for a team failing, particularly in the early phases of its lifecycle.

Critical areas to watch out for that can cause teams to become dysfunctional are defined by Lenciono[7]:

- inattention to results
- avoidance of accountability
- lack of commitment
- fear of conflict, and
- absence of trust

The journey of a team is not a smooth continuum. A team can easily split into factions or 'splinters' particularly when teams change their membership, have diversity issues and or face adversity. Splinters can cause conflict, relationship clashes and trigger other behaviours that are destructive and will impair the team's performance. As a leader, be on your guard at these vulnerable points in the team's journey.

Team Exercise: Why teams fail

As a team, review the reasons why teams fail and ask each member to give a 'danger rating' to each category, for your team. For example, using a 'RAG' ⌴ status rate each as 'Red', 'Amber' or 'Green'.

Look at the mix of team responses for each category. How consistent are they?

Discuss each category and form a consensus view as to its 'danger rating'.

Look at the mix of green versus red and amber across all the categories.

Is the team clear on any root causes of any red or amber ratings? Are there any data or measurements that support these views?

What actions are needed to address any red or amber ratings?

Repeat this process at regular intervals, and specifically when there are major changes to ensure that you keep pace with changes in facts, perceptions and feelings.

Effectiveness Tips:

✓ Identify the signals of failing teams and take action to combat any that are relevant to your team

✓ Be aware when forming a new team, or when new members join, that not everyone may be skilled in teamworking

✓ Be mindful of the potential impact of the organisation's reward system on effective teamwork

✓ Watch out for splinters

2 Direction

The effective team uses the vision, mission, values and principles, goals, priorities and objectives of its stakeholders to set its direction.

To move in this direction, the team shares a common identity and sense of mission and unites around common goals, objectives and priorities.

Effective Team Characteristic 9:
Has a common sense of identity, purpose and principles

In order to be effective, a team needs a common sense of identity, purpose and principles.

A common identity and purpose includes a common team:

- Mission
- Vision
- Brand
- Set of Values
- Set of Principles and Beliefs

You should use team building activities to agree and subsequently reaffirm a common team view, understanding and commitment to the above.

In agreeing your team's vision, mission, values, beliefs and principles, you and your team should ensure that you are aligned to those of the wider organisation and stakeholders – as the team exists to meet their needs.

Identity

Do you and your team know who you are? The answer may not be as obvious as it appears on the surface. Having a clear sense of identity is important to a team and how the team is known often starts with the team name. People generally prefer to belong to something that they can name.

Team Exercise: Our identity

As a team, discuss the following:

- Compare the name of the team as known in the organisation with the name of the team as seen by the team.

- How well does each reflect 'what we actually do'?

- If either name doesn't accurately describe 'what we actually do', what might this mean for our stakeholders? Are we fully aligned to their needs? Are they aware of the full extent of what we can do for them?

- How does each name reflect the uniqueness of this team and differentiate it from others?

- What is the significance of that difference?

- Is there enough differentiation to help our stakeholders understand what we can do for them?

Purpose

Once you and your team have agreed a clear name that is meaningful to you and to other key stakeholders, the next step is to define the purpose of the team. What is the team there to do?

The mission statement articulates why the team exists. In many cases it stands on its own merits and is presented separately to any other team identity statement. In some cases a statement on the future, often called a vision statement, is integrated with the mission statement into one statement of intent.

As a leader, the wording of your mission statement matters, as it needs to articulate your unique purpose accurately, clearly and crisply to a range of stakeholders. A confused mission statement will not provide the clarity of focus that an effective team needs in order to develop.

Team Exercise: Our purpose

Following on from the Identity exercise, ask the team:

- Why do we exist?

After all the jokes that usually result at this point, ask the team to think about why they are sanctioned to exist in the company.

- What is driving the need?

- Who says we need this team and why?

- Use these answers to create a clear mission or purpose statement

- Circulate it to your key stakeholders to see if it resonates with them and their expectations. Does it make sense to them?

- Produce a final statement and circulate it to the team

There is a trap with creating mission statements that is best avoided. Team members can become impatient with the process and feel that at times too much painstaking attention is being paid to the detail of each word. However, it is vital that you get this statement right as it will stay with the team for a long time and will form the team's foundation, upon which its values, principles and objectives will be built. Take care not to waste time on excessive 'wordsmithing' that makes no substantive change to the meaning of the statement, rather spend time gaining consensus on a statement that can last and be believed in.

The other danger that afflicts a team mission's statement is that it becomes passive and ends up on paper but nowhere else. Take care to ensure that your mission statement is alive in documentation, planning and when setting objectives. Review its relevance when your deliverables, processes or the organisation changes.

Brand

The questions on mission stimulate team discussions that can be used to form a common view of the team's identity. They also begin to build a foundation for developing a team 'brand'.

A team's brand is essentially a promise. It embodies its commitments to its stakeholders and reflects the emotions and perceptions that comprise stakeholder satisfaction.

Team Exercise: Our brand

Working with the team, explore the following:

- Do we have a brand that can be identified?

- What are the 'promises' that typify our brand?

- If asked, how would our customers and other stakeholders describe our brand?

- What are the physical and emotional aspects, features and benefits that stakeholders use to describe the brand?

Exploring these questions in depth encourages a team to examine itself and what it has to offer. The process should help the team identify the perceptions and emotions that comprise the stakeholder's view of their performance.

Ultimately, the brand embodies and communicates the team's identity, vision and mission. It must resonate with the team and make it instantly recognisable to, and set an expectation with, key stakeholders and the wider organisation.

Values

Many organisations have a stated set of values that they regard as fundamental to the way they operate. Values are the basic convictions of what is important. They reflect either end states or ways of working that are preferred compared to others.

Meaningful values resonate with identity and brand. They support the behaviours to be used to achieve the organisation's purpose. They tend to be expressed as one-word statements, although they sometimes include a short explanation.

Examples of the publicly stated values of several international 'blue -chip' organisations include:

- Integrity
- Irrepressible
- Inviting
- Openness
- Passionate
- Accountability
- Boldness
- Innovative
- Respect
- Fun

Whatever an organisation's values, these will be the values that it will expect your team to share as an integrated part of the whole. If the organisation's values are not embodied in all of its day to day operations, they remain mere words that cannot create the desired positive impact on its results.

Depending on the needs of your team, you might add some supplemental values to reflect the way the team needs to perform in your local environment. Of course, these will have to support the shared corporate values.

Team Exercise: Values

Working as a team, develop some creative ideas of what values are important to the team and why.

Refine the list into 4 to 6 key values that you will use day to day to guide all activity, in addition to your organisation's values.

Are these the same as the values of your organisation? Explore any differences and assess whether they could impact the team's alignment to the delivery of stakeholder needs.

Like all of the elements of Direction, it can be easy to create well-written statements and then leave them on the shelf.

The power of these statements to positively impact the team's results lie with the statements themselves, the team members' shared attachment to them and the way that they bring them to life in their activities every day.

As a leader, ensure that you model your organisation's values and any additional team values that you have agreed. Monitor the everyday attitudes and behaviours demonstrated by the team and use positive reinforcement to embed the values in the way you work.

Leader Exercise: Assess whether values are used

One way to encourage your team to live the values is to formally link their use to your assessment of how well they have delivered their performance objectives.

When reviewing performance, document examples of when the use of the values was demonstrated in the delivery of the objectives. Note any examples of when the values were not supported or demonstrated. In completing the performance appraisal, give appropriate weight to the degree that the values were evident as part of the individual's overall delivery.

From these findings recognise and reward great behaviour.

Discuss as part of the appraisal, and if required, agree changes in behaviour that will improve the demonstration of the values. Take action on behaviour that conflicts with the values.

Document the key findings. Use them as the basis for future discussions.

In general, are the values alive in the way that the team generally works? If this could be improved, how could you encourage this in a way that is engaging, rather than creating cynicism?

Shared principles and beliefs

Some organisations define their business principles. These principles are sometimes a combination of high level goals such as 'creating wealth', high level corporate values such as 'trust' or 'diversity', responsibilities towards stakeholders and occasionally, lower level value statements like 'being innovative'.

These statements are often presented in the form of a short 'statement of principle' with two or three lines of text developing the rationale.

Some examples of actual statements of corporate principles are:

Our goal is to provide superior returns to our shareholders;
Delivering sustainable superior returns and profitability is critical and substantial stock ownership for our employees will align our employees with our shareholders.

And

We aim to deliver sustainable business development;
Sustainability development is critical for our long term success and will require the balancing of short and long term priorities in our decision making that balance the needs of all our stakeholders.

Sometimes these principles go further, for example:

Principle: Business Integrity;
We will operate in an open, fair and honest manner in all our dealings and aspects of business. We will expect that all those who deal with us will act in the same way. We will avoid conflicts of interest and will require our employees to declare any potential conflicts.

This statement is a principle that takes a certain ethical position.

Another business principle addresses regulatory needs and compliance requirements:

Principle: Compliance and Regulatory Adherence;
We will comply with all regulatory and statutory and legal laws, regulations and requirements in all aspects of our business.

As can be seen, these principles and stated beliefs are different to values. Values are a short, often one word statement fundamental to the culture and the operation of the business. The principle is a longer statement setting out intent and rationale.

Many companies that publish their principles wrap them up in one document alongside their values so that they can be read together.

Principles can be very powerful as a strong foundation upon which to build the business. They are a clear declaration of intent and working parameters, and a clear signal to the staff and other stakeholders of what guides the organisation's behaviour and decision making.

Not all companies have gone as far as to declare their principles. If your company has, you should reinforce these principles in your team on a regular basis to maintain awareness and promote ways of working that are in line with the organisation's intent.

In line with many other similar statements, the principles can get lost in the hurly burly of day to day activity and thus forgotten. In some extreme cases the way others, for example, suppliers wish to operate may challenge the principles. If this is the case you must stay with the principles and ensure that there are mechanisms to raise these dilemmas for resolution.

Even if your organisation has a set of principles, it is useful to get your team to define what principles are important to guide and govern their operation day to day. As with the corporate principles these team principles can be an effective way to set expectations of behaviours and ways of working that align with the needs of the organisation. In this way, the principles can be very powerful as a means of contributing to stakeholder satisfaction and therefore Team Effectiveness.

An effective team has a strongly held common view of the basic principles and purpose that underpin their existence and performance.

Teams can of course exist without this bond, but the stronger the bond, the stronger the foundation for the team to develop high performance.

The shared parameters that contribute to building this foundation include:

- A strong sense of purpose, often typified by a clear statement of mission or 'the business this team is in is....'

- A clear, articulated vision of the future that the team is aiming for

- A strong brand identity which resonates with the team and other stakeholders

- Team values, documented and used to underpin performance and behaviour

- The underlying principles and beliefs that the team expect will be evident in the team members' day-to-day activities and ways of working.

Team Exercise: Principles

- If the organisation has stated principles, discuss them with the team and discuss how they guide performance day to day

- As a team, brainstorm the most important principles that govern the way you work. Rationalise these by gaining consensus on the top 3 to 5, carefully explaining why these are more important than those that you have de-prioritised

- Document these principles and their rationale

- Share the final principles with key stakeholders and communicate them to other relevant parties

- Bring the principles alive in documents, processes and behaviours. Measure actual behaviours against them

- Regularly review the principles for consistency with those of the organisation, particularly in times of organisational change

Effectiveness Tips:

✓ Have a shared sense of identity, purpose, values and principles

✓ Ensure that these support the mission, values and principles of the wider organisation

✓ Use positive reinforcement to strengthen the team's association with these concepts and embed them into your identity, culture and ways of working

Effective Team Characteristic 10:
Has clear common goals, objectives and priorities

The team is of course there to deliver a defined set of outputs for its stakeholders.

An organisation's goals define how its high level aims captured in its vision will be achieved. The goals are achieved by shorter term objectives that are specific and measureable. The objectives provide stepping stones to the achievement of the goals. A simple example would be the vision of an athlete to be regarded as the greatest athlete in the world. In order to achieve that vision, the goal is to win both the Olympics and the World Championships. As the athlete is only 12 years' old, this year's objective is to win at the school championships.

To be effective, a team needs clear, common goals and objectives and agreed strategies for delivery. To ensure that these are the right goals to focus the team's efforts and resources to achieve the right outcomes, the team needs to align and integrate its plans with those of the organisation.

The team needs to know the organisation's objectives and understand how its own objectives, plans, targets and budgets contribute to achieving the overall result. This enables the team to focus on a 'greater purpose' and on tailoring its output to best deliver it. This can be illustrated by the example of the craftsman observed working on a brick. When asked, what he is doing, he answers 'building a cathedral!' Of course, he could also have said 'making a brick' but he was clearly aligned to the overall objective and was focusing his efforts accordingly!

The effective team has clear sight of the bigger picture and pride and ownership in its part in delivering it.

As a team, work through a systematic process to align your plans with those of your stakeholders.

Your plans should include the following elements:

- Strategic Goals
- Key Result Areas
- Critical Success Factors
- Objectives
- Targets
- Initiatives
- Accountability and Responsibility
- Time-frames

These are normally formatted around a Balanced Scorecard.

Most organisations will have some form of planning and budgeting process. This process will aim to cascade the strategic goals down to actions at the local level. Some organisations have an iterative process where bottom up and top down considerations combine to produce the objectives and targets.

Even if your organisation has a strong goal alignment process it is important that you as a leader use the checklist above to ensure that your final goals and plan map to each corresponding element in the organisation's overall plans. The team goals will also map across to each individual's own personal objectives and annual performance goals.

Alignment of goals, objectives and priorities from the wider business through the team to the individual will greatly assist focused effort and effective delivery of results for stakeholders.

Team Exercise: Goal alignment and objectives setting

Schedule time with your team for an objectives setting session (or review session if you need it during the year).

To ensure that everyone has a common understanding of both the organisation's and the team's goals, work through the following together.

Start with a refresh of the mission and vision to ground the exercise.

- Is the organisation's vision clear and is everyone in the team aware and aligned to it?

- Is our vision and how it supports the vision of the wider organisation clear?

- Is our purpose clear and understood by everyone?

- Are the organisation's strategic goals that achieve the vision understood? Do we understand how our goals contribute to their delivery?

- Do we know the urgency of the strategic imperatives i.e. the critical strategic needs of the organisation as a whole?

- Do we know the stakeholders and a Balanced Scorecard[13] type of view of this stakeholder landscape?

- Do we understand what is critical to achieve and is it clearly articulated?

- Are the objectives clearly stated and communicated?

Team Exercise: Goal alignment and objectives setting

- Are the team's and each individual's objectives SMART (Specific, Measurable, Achievable, Realistic, Time bound)?

- Do we know how the objectives translate into specific performance targets and Key Performance Indicators?

- Do we know the timeframes for each specific target i.e. what must be achieved this quarter, this year?

- Do the targets reflect seasonality and actual business trading conditions, for example, customer contact fluctuations?

- Are initiatives, programmes, projects and business as usual efforts clearly mapped and assigned to the delivery of specific objectives?

- Are accountabilities and responsibilities assigned to deliverables?

- Are the mechanisms for reviewing progress detailed and understood by all?

- Is the process for creating the plan known and are the right people involved in the creation and approval of the plan, including all stakeholders?

- Is the process for formally changing the plan during the year and accountabilities, responsibilities and the authority for this defined?

- Does the whole team agree that that they have responsibility for making this plan work as well as raising issues with it to improve it and team's ability to deliver it?

A checklist template to help you with preparing and aligning your plans:

	Are the strategies, goals, objectives and plans clear?
1	The organisation's vision is
2	Our vision is
3	The organisation's strategies are
4	The organisation's goals are
5	The team's objectives are
6	Our objectives are SMART
7	Our objectives clearly link to initiatives
8	Our objectives have time sequenced targets
9	Accountabilities and responsibilities are allocated to the objectives
10	We review progress to plan every...
11	We review progress to plan in the following way...
12	Accountability for delivery of the plan rests with...
13	Responsibility for making this plan work rests with...
14	Issues with this plan are escalated to ...
15	The budget is aligned and follows the above principles
16	The budget delivers the plan
17	The budget and the plan are approved

Urgent and Important

Things change! The team needs to react. The team has its plans, budgets and targets. But, things seem to change every day. Everyday someone comes up with another urgent need: 'drop everything, do this!', 'I need this now!' and 'when can you do this?'

In some circumstances these urgent needs reflect the realities of running complex businesses and processes, dealing with increasingly competitive market conditions, financial pressures and changing customer needs. In other cases they are the result of other teams, leaders, managers and units not in control or acting in a well-planned, constructive or cohesive manner. Whatever the cause, the team needs to flex and deal with the reality of changing customer and stakeholder needs.

To help do this the team needs to keep under constant review what is urgent and what is important. These priorities will constantly change.

Some leaders say that this is obvious and just dismiss this idea as 'common sense'. But, in my experience, when many leaders are asked to be specific as to what is actually urgent and important, they often find it hard to do so apart from the top three items. These may barely describe the full extent of the team's workload, the strain on resources and prioritisation dilemmas.

To help juggle complex, competing demands, is it is often very useful to display current tasks, activities and initiatives on an Urgent - Important Grid.[14]

This simple tool can help the team communicate and track how tasks move around and enter the field of play as the year progresses. Having one view helps keeps everyone on track and aligned with changing priorities.

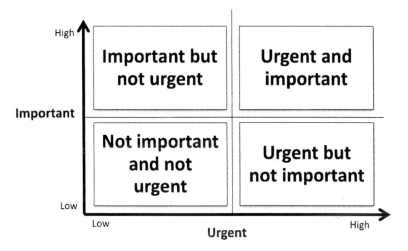

Figure 4 The Urgent-Important Grid

Team Exercise: The Urgent-Important Grid[14]

In discussion with the team, place initiatives, projects or tasks on the grid. Draw a ball on the grid to represent each.

Size the ball by some agreed criteria that represent the size of task. For example, budget allocated, number of people or man hours involved, benefits to be delivered etc.

Keep the grid under review with other forms of plan presentation.

Place new tasks onto the grid as they arrive and retire completed tasks.

Keep old versions to show what has been achieved over time or over a year.

Use your grid to discuss the impact of new issues on workload with stakeholders and whether the team can actually deliver on everything with its current resources.

Use the grid to monitor what is consuming resources and challenge why.

Effectiveness Tips:

✓ Have clear, common goals, objectives and priorities

✓ Make sure that the team understands how these deliver the vision and strategic goals of the wider organisation

✓ Make sure that the team has a common, up to date view on what is urgent and what is important

✓ Use the Urgent-Important Grid to monitor and balance urgent short term demands and priorities against annual or longer term objectives

Effective Team Characteristic 11:
Knows its stakeholders

To be an effective, a team needs to know who is judging its performance.

In larger organisations the interplay of stakeholders can be very complex. So many people seemingly with something to say and so many with a stake in performance.

Effective teams distil these forces and are clear on what is needed to satisfy the stakeholders who are impacted by, and are interested in, their performance.

When teams are asked to list their stakeholders, this can actually be a far more complex exercise than it first appears. Each high level stakeholder may have a number of different facets, each facet having their own or even, unhelpfully, conflicting needs. For example, if another department in your organisation is a key stakeholder, you will need to isolate each key relationship your team has with this department and treat each as a separate stakeholder, with separate needs.

This will be important to do in cases where each of these relationships is producing a different level of satisfaction for the stakeholder. In the example given above, this could be a case where the middle management layer has a completely different working relationship and level of stakeholder satisfaction to say, the leadership level.

Therefore, to manage your stakeholders effectively, each group or in some cases specific individuals need to be treated separately. This is rather like a marketing segmentation exercise where the aim is to understand specific groups with specific needs and not treat everyone the same.

This is important in order to understand who the stakeholders are, build relationships and critically, to understand the specific needs and requirements of each. In order to meet those needs, you will have to work with your stakeholders to define outputs and agree measures of performance. This process cannot happen if you are unclear as to whom your stakeholders are.

The prime stakeholder groups at the organisational level are usually defined as:

- Shareholders
- Customers
- People
- Suppliers
- Community, including regulatory bodies

Each group has its own set of needs and their delivery is measured at the organisational level. You will need to be aware of those measurements and how your team's performance contributes to them. This isn't always as simple as it sounds. It may be difficult for front line or support teams to associate with measures at the organisational level, such as (external) 'Customer Satisfaction' or 'Return on Capital'.

The stakeholder needs will also compete and sometimes it will seem difficult to satisfy competing demands. Understanding stakeholder needs in these circumstances is even more critical in order to prioritise and focus team activity.

Remember, as well as the obvious stakeholders of your value chain there are people who interact with and support your team from a wide variety of functions in the business. These groups will also have requirements of your team and form perceptions of your team's effectiveness. These groups can also influence the perception of your performance across the wider organisation.

Be conscious to identify the needs of these groups (and what you require from them) within your team's business plans, goals and objectives.

Leader Exercise: Know your stakeholders

1. To provide context, identify stakeholders as defined by your organisation (for example, in its Annual Report).

2. For alignment, identify the stakeholders (and or Balanced Scorecard categories) of the leadership level above your team.

3. List your stakeholders using the primary headings: Shareholder, Customers, People, Suppliers and Community as a guide, and or using any Balanced Scorecard type approach used in your organisation.

4. Break these high level headings down into specific units, teams and people.

Use the list as the basis for relationship building and agreeing measures of performance.

Map these stakeholders to your goals and objective setting process. Align the goals to stakeholder needs and use this to determine the importance of each objective (High, Medium, Low).

Ensure that you agree with each stakeholder clearly defined and measurable outputs to enable both parties to evaluate performance.

Do your answers highlight any opportunities for you to increase your understanding of, and improve these relationships and your team's effectiveness?

Leader Exercise: Know your stakeholders (continued)

Use the following checklist to help you complete the exercise on the previous page.

Who are the people, groups and teams that:

- are the suppliers and support units that provide you with information, data, goods and services as part of their outputs?

- represent the shareholders' needs for efficient and effective delivery at lowest cost?

- represent customer views and feedback?

- represent the views, issues, concerns and aspirations of the team itself and the other people that work in the organisation?

- represent the community you work within?

- represent the regulatory, legal and risk requirements for the work your team performs?

- represent change requirements and needs?

Assess how strong you think your relationship with each party is. How well do you know each of their needs and agendas?

Do your answers highlight any opportunities for you to increase your understanding of, and improve these relationships and your team's effectiveness?

Create a simple template along the lines below to capture your answers:

Who are our stakeholders?		
1	Our stakeholders are	
2	Those who rely on us are	
3	Those that enable our performance are	
4	Those that support us are	

Effectiveness Tips:
✓ Know your stakeholders and ensure that you have defined with them how your outputs and their satisfaction will be measured

3 Structure

The effective team knows how it fits into and how it is influenced by the structures of its organisation.

It understands and acquires the competencies required and the quantum of resources needed to meet its goals.

It structures its talents, skills and resources in the most effective way to deliver its goals and objectives.

Effective Team Characteristic 12:
Knows how it fits into the wider organisation

An effective team understands how they fit with:

- the structures of the organisation
- the governance of the organisation
- the structures of the local unit or department
- other similarly configured teams

Knowing who you are is vital and so is being very clear about how you fit within the wider framework of the organisation.

Each organisation has governance frameworks including committees, boards, management meetings or other authority groupings. An effective team understands and can see these other structures in relation to themselves.

An effective team knows how these groups influence the team, set agendas and goals and in turn, understands how they influence these groups.

To be effective, a team must understand the autonomy that goes with its position in the organisation's structures and what is expected of it. A lack of organisational and governance awareness will prevent a team from fully understanding its role and how others will judge its performance.

It is often surprising to find team members who do not understand the interplay of the influence of other team structures. They can even be unaware of what other teams (and their agendas) exist around them, except for those that they immediately interact with. A classic example of this is where teams sit metres away from each other and never interact in a meaningful way, or just send each other emails.

A team is better placed if it understands the other teams around it. It can then learn from their perceptions, results and experiences and use this knowledge to develop and improve their performance.

Team Exercise: How do you fit?

Work through the following questions with your team to check that everyone understands where the team fits.

- What does the organisation chart show about where this team fits? Is it correct, up to date and does it reflect reality?

- How visible is this team within the wider organisation chart? Is it visible to others or buried in generic headings and losing its identity at certain levels?

- Outside of the organisation chart, what are the governance structures that sit around this team that manage or assess its performance?

- Outside of the organisation chart, what governance or other structures manage and influence change that could impact this team?

- How does this team fit with other teams that may perform similar functions?

- If there are teams that perform similar functions how is this team identified and governed. How is it the same or different to the others?

- What are the informal governance structures that affect this team?

A checklist template to help you with 'Knowing how we fit?'

How do we fit?		
1	How is the unit shown on the lowest level of the organisation chart?	
2	How is the team shown on the unit or department chart?	
3	How is the team shown on the high level organisational chart?	
4	What are the key related organisational charts?	
5	What do these charts tell us about how we see ourselves and how others see us or know about us?	
6	What are the important governance structures that impact us?	
7	Are there teams that fit in the organisation in a similar way to us, that others view as identical?	
8	If this is the case, how do we differentiate ourselves?	
9	Describe how we fit and feature in the organisation's governance	

Effectiveness Tips:

✓ Know how you fit to improve the delivery of stakeholder satisfaction and perceptions

✓ Ensure that you are aware of all groups and structures that can impact, or who will assess your team's performance

✓ Interact more effectively with other value chains in the organisation. See where you can contribute more. See what you can learn

Effective Team Characteristic 13: Knows who does what and why

Effective teams have a strong appreciation of each role in the team and how it contributes to the effectiveness of the team's overall delivery.

Roles are much more than job titles, which can often give just a high level impression of the role. A job title on its own is usually not enough to give you insight into the scope of a person's responsibilities and their contribution to delivering the unit's or organisation's objectives at a detailed level.

Outside of formal job titles, people may assume roles within a team that suit their skills, experience, strengths and personality. Some people are extroverted and may want to chair meetings or act as facilitators. Some people are introverted and may prefer to undertake research. Another example is a team where each member has the same title, for instance, 'Customer Service Officer.' In this case, each person might have different specific responsibilities or accountabilities, such as 'Project Lead', 'Employee Engagement Champion', 'Communication Coordinator' or 'Risk Assessor.

An effective team understands the roles people play and how they switch in and out of roles day to day with different accountabilities and responsibilities.

This can be a complex dynamic but is an area that can make a team shine as they can use each other's competencies to their best advantage, complement each other and reduce the potential for turf wars or personal disputes.

Effective teams have almost a sixth sense about how team members will take on roles. They make best use of natural preferences when allocating responsibilities and accountabilities.

Effective teams develop a common view of the preferences of team members: who is responsible and accountable formally and informally for what. They are good at communicating around these subjects and can openly challenge and offer up different combinations of the team to increase effectiveness.

Another important perspective on the types of role people undertake in a team focuses on our natural, personal 'tendency to behave, contribute and interrelate with others in a particular way.' Dr Meredith Belbin[15] developed this concept and identified Nine Team Roles ⌣ (also known as Belbin's® Team Roles) that individuals display to varying degrees.

These are set out in the table below.

Role	Description
1. Plant	Creative in problem solving
2. Monitor Evaluator	Logical and impartial
3. Coordinator	Focuses on the objective and drawing people out
4. Resource Investigator	Examines the world outside and makes sure that team ideas work
5. Implementer	Plans and implements efficiently
6. Completer Finisher	Adds polish at the end of tasks, scrutinises for error and delivers high quality control
7. Teamworker	Gets team to gel, identifies work required, 'does it' for the team
8. Shaper	Provides drive, keeps team moving
9. Specialist	Provides in-depth knowledge

Each of these roles has its strengths and weaknesses. Each of the role behaviours is needed to make a team successful in all stages of its lifecycle. Belbin's key message is that a balance of all roles is needed within a team.

Having a predominance of one or several role types or lacking role types will limit a team's effectiveness. As an example, a team with no shapers can end up directionless and miss deadlines. Teams with too many shapers can in-fight about direction and can stall due to a lack of consensus.

Team roles can be identified using Belbin's 'Self Perception Inventory'[15].

Other writers also identify behavioural role preferences. Many of us will have experienced working in teams where the balance of roles performed produces ineffective performance.

We can all perform each role and do so. However, we have a natural preference for some particular roles.

As a leader, it is useful to understand the role preferences in your team and how they are influencing team behaviour and outcomes. Belbin's role preferences result in certain observable behaviours as set out in the table above. As behaviour is observable, it can be measured, discussed, used as feedback and changed. As Belbin points out, behaviours are the most significant difference between a team's success and failure, far more than the intellect of its members.

As a leader, you can use your team's role preferences to help allocate work and responsibilities in accordance with an individual's strengths or in order to develop their capabilities. If the natural tendencies of your team look unbalanced, you could use different techniques to build the role behaviours that are less represented.

In specific cases, for example when undertaking a major project, you could also bring in additional people to supplement missing or weaker role types to increase the overall team's effectiveness.

Team Exercise: Role clarity

Examine your team for clarity of:

- Role title
- Accountabilities
- Responsibilities
- Informal roles
- Roles interacting with other teams
- Authority levels by role

Discuss these with the team. Develop mutual understanding and respect of what each team member does. This activity is useful to do when setting the team's goals and objectives or when planning a major project.

You could also consider asking the team to complete Belbin's 'Self Perception Inventory' and use the results to examine the balance of natural role preferences within the team. This may provide some insight into how the team's effectiveness could be improved, either by allocating work to people with complimentary natural tendencies or supplementing any role preferences that might be lacking.

Effectiveness Tips:

✓ Have a common view across the team of roles and responsibilities – and their rationale

✓ Use Belbin or other team behavioural role questionnaires to assess the balance of roles within your team

✓ Use natural tendencies to your advantage; coach and provide support to assist people complete tasks that do not suit their behavioural role preferences

4 Value

The effective team knows the value it is adding to the organisation's inputs, processes, outputs and outcomes.

It is clear about its product and service offering and the needs of the customers that use its outputs.

It manages its processes to be effective and efficient and focuses its efforts on activities that are of value to its stakeholders.

It uses effective measures and clarity around variation to direct and objectively evaluate its performance, the performance of its processes and the satisfaction of its stakeholders.

Effective Team Characteristic 14:
Knows its value chain and its requirements

Teams need to be clear on who they are and how they fit in order to position themselves successfully in the organisational context.

In order to be effective, teams will also need an agreed and understood view of the organisational framework in which they operate. This means understanding and being able to describe their:

- Suppliers, internal and external
- Customers, internal and external
- Processes
- Supporters or enablers of performance
- Outputs
- Outcomes

This analysis defines the core set of processes that a team conducts and the transformations of inputs to outputs that they perform. It defines the work performed and the value that is added by the team. With this clarity and understanding the team can begin to analyse and improve its process performance. This analysis also specifies the outputs and outcomes required from the work undertaken. It defines boundaries of activity and the interfaces the team has with other processes.

A technique called a SIPOC diagram ⌞⌟ presents a useful high level view of the sequence from suppliers through a transformation process to end customers.

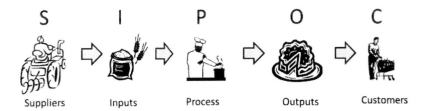

S   **I**   **P**   **O**   **C**

Suppliers   Inputs   Process   Outputs   Customers

Figure 5 Supplier, Inputs, Process, Outputs, Customer (SIPOC) diagram

Team Exercise: Document your value chain

Work through the following questions with your team to create a SIPOC diagram. Ensure that everyone takes away a clear understanding of the team's value chain.

- Who are your suppliers? Are they internal or external to the organisation, unit or department?

- What do these suppliers provide in terms of physical inputs, goods, services or information and support?

- How are these products or services provided?

- What are the important inputs that the team receives?

- What are the high level prime processes that the team performs?

- How would you describe that transformation process i.e. what is transformed into what?

- What are the outputs from the transformation process?

- What form do these outputs take?

- How do these outputs reach the customer?

- Who are the customers?

- Are these customers (at a high level) segmented?

- Are these customers in one place or dispersed?

- What need are we trying to satisfy by providing these outputs to the customer?

- What 'higher cause' is served by the customer having the outputs?

Use this simple form to capture the results of the exercise.

Value Chain Checklist		
1	Our suppliers are	
2	The inputs we receive are	
3	Our primary processes that transform the inputs are	
4	The key outputs that we deliver are	
5	Our key customers are	
6	Our processes form part of the following other larger processes	
7	For our processes to be successful, we need the following enabling processes to perform effectively	
8	The customer's needs that are met from the receipt of our outputs are	
9	The customer can achieve the following higher level need or cause by receiving our outputs	

Effectiveness Tips:

✓ Know your value chain. Maintain a SIPOC diagram and map critical processes

✓ Use the value chain to define the scope of the team's activities and understand the value added by your processes. Use this understanding as the foundation for process improvement activity

✓ Use the value chain to ensure that you have clarity on expected outputs and outcomes

Effective Team Characteristic 15:
Knows its processes and systems

Processes are the real time flow of people, materials, information and knowledge that transform inputs into products and services for customers.

Each team provides a specific contribution to the organisation's processes. Some teams manage low level business processes that fit entirely within their remit. Some teams are part of major customer facing processes. Some see the business process end to end while some are a single cog in a more elaborate chain. Wherever we are in the organisation, we are all part of and perform processes.

An effective team understands its position in, and contribution to, the business processes. They can clearly articulate:

- The inputs they receive
- The core processes they undertake
- The support processes that are needed to make their team function effectively and efficiently
- The transformations that occur when they undertake their processes
- The outputs they produce
- The outcomes the customer is seeking from their outputs
- Their own processes, in order to continuously challenge their effectiveness and efficiency and implement improvements

Using the stakeholder 'know where you fit' and SIPOC analyses covered earlier, the team should be clear on both its position in the organisation and in its end to end processes.

Using the SIPOC analysis as a base, you can now develop a more detailed definition and breakdown of each process the team is responsible for.

This next layer of detail should focus on how work actually gets done and highlight both problems and opportunities for improvement. Critically assessing the flow of work may generate suggestions for improvement.

The effective team knows how it uses:

- Processes
- Activities
- Tasks
- Work Instructions
- Procedures
- Guidelines
- Rules and Regulations

to govern the functioning and performance of its processes. It keeps them in view and reviews them regularly.

Technology is a critical enabler of most processes. It is interesting to see how often people demonstrate little understanding of the technology infrastructure essential to their performance or that could significantly impact their roles and processes if it were to change. In order to understand and manage its processes effectively, a team needs to know what systems they depend on to deliver their stakeholder needs and have contingency plans in place in case they fail. As a result, ensure that any technologies and systems supporting your processes are clear on any process maps.

The effective team also needs to know how any proposed process improvements will impact their systems and whether they will require a change in technology.

In reverse, they will also need to know and manage the impact of any planned technology changes on their processes. In both cases, the impact of process and or technology changes on people will obviously have to be managed carefully and sensitively.

Effectiveness Tips:

✓ Know your processes and systems at a detailed level in order to understand the root causes of issues and to spot opportunities for improvement

✓ Understand the role technology plays in your ability to deliver your objectives. Ensure that you have a contingency plan in place in case it fails

✓ Understand how changes in your processes will impact technology and vice versa

✓ The impact on people of any proposed changes in processes or technology needs to be managed carefully and sensitively

Effective Team Characteristic 16:
Knows its products and services and what is expected

It almost seems too simple to state that people should know their products and services. Surprisingly, sometimes this isn't all that clear to everyone.

Sometimes teams perform a multitude of similar tasks flipping from one inbound enquiry to another. Sometimes teams are specialists partnering the business or are a support function dealing with many varied requests and needs for information.

Teams have many priorities and functions as we know. Ask your team:

- What are the products we produce?
- What are the services we deliver?

See what comes back. Do you get answers that are high level and generic such as 'We provide good customer service' or 'We deliver whatever analysis the customer unit needs'. If so, is this good enough?

Many teams, particularly where their product or service is intangible and 'soft' such as information, knowledge or experience often lack a common view when answering these simple questions. This is because the team tends to spend so much of its time responding to customer enquiries and requests that can vary widely in their nature, urgency and importance.

Effective teams know what they are delivering and why it is important to the customer. Their products and services have agreed specifications that allow stakeholder satisfaction to be measured objectively.

This allows the team to focus its combined efforts and resources to deliver to specification, minimising defects, waste and time spent on activity that has no value to the customer.

The simple act of discussing these questions and agreeing written answers, which can act as a touchstone, raises the awareness of outputs and keeps everyone focused.

Effectiveness Tips:

✓ Know what products and services you are delivering and why they are important to the customer

✓ Use this to focus the team's activity on what is of value to the customer

✓ Ensure that the team has a strong understanding of the detailed specifications for the output and how customer satisfaction will be measured

A checklist template to help you define your products and services:

	What are our products and services?	
1	The primary products we produce are	
2	Additional products are...	
3	The primary services we deliver are...	
4	Additional services are...	
5	The most important features for our customers are	
6	Additional features for our customers are	
7	The prime beneficiary of our products and services is	
8	Other beneficiaries of our services are...	
9	The most important benefit derived by our customers for the product or service are	
10	Additional benefits are	
11	The design and delivery of our products and services meets customer needs	

5 Improvement

The effective team has a strong improvement focus. It identifies problems and opportunities and executes improvements based on facts. It uses structured processes and management techniques for problem solving and to implement change. It unleashes ideas, creativity and innovation.

It makes clear decisions with strong decision making processes.

Proposals for change and investment are made and evaluated using standard criteria.

Effective Team Characteristic 17: Unleashes Creativity and Ideas

Effective teams value and actively work to unleash the creativity and innovation of team members.

Creativity and innovation have become more of a need as the pace of change and the complexity of issues facing organisations increases. Current thinking, processes and approaches no longer always deliver the best results.

Processes need to consistently perform for the customer. They also need to adapt to the changing dynamics of customers' and stakeholders' needs. Maintaining outputs that meet customers' requirements first time every time is a need. Managing this, as well as being able to effectively respond to changing supplier, process, employee and technology needs, is likely to require creativity. Solutions to new issues or new combinations of old issues require creativity. Doing more to beat the competition requires creativity and innovation.

Effective teams must therefore manage two competing forces: maintaining the consistency and capability of output whilst being creative and innovative. This can challenge even the best of teams.

To achieve this, the team needs to use strong process management to ensure that each process delivers to agreed specifications and requirements. Alongside this, the team needs to use separate, more creative techniques for process improvement. Improvements are then implemented into 'business as usual' processes and process improvement activity starts again. This is a cycle and teams need to recognise the different skills needed in each phase and ensure that they overtly manage both processes.

Creativity doesn't just happen - the conditions that encourage creativity and innovation need to be in place.

Teams that use structured problem solving and process improvement methodologies can find themselves being creative and innovative in a focused, measured and resourced manner.

Within a project structure or problem solving process, a number of tools and techniques can be used to solicit ideas and develop creative solutions. These include trials and pilots to test if proposed ideas and improvements are feasible before investing heavily in them and developing them to scale. Using formal governance procedures to launch projects and secure funding is an important aspect of delivering change.

There are some schools of thought that think teams need complete 'freedom' or 'no rules' to be creative. This is far from the case as such teams can develop norms of behaviour that do not allow creativity to blossom. It can be far more effective to facilitate structured processes for one or many participants as a great enabler for generating ideas.

Creativity also flows in a team when a team is needed. That means that if an idea is best developed by the team, get the team into action. If it is better for an individual with expertise and experience to develop an idea, don't force a team onto the problem.

Learn creative tools and techniques and use them. Some good examples are: Brainstorming, Affinity Diagrams, Channelling and SCAMPER.

Do not play with them. Use them as they are designed and inside structured processes.

Suggestions

How many suggestions for improvement does your team generate?

Is it a vibrant team using team briefings and meetings to generate new ideas? Does it generate so many ideas that they are never followed up? Or are people reluctant to suggest new ideas because they are happy with the status quo?

If every team meeting generated a flood of new ideas and suggestions, it would be difficult to get anything done! However, effective teams draw on the creative resources and ideas at their disposal in a focused and disciplined way to achieve their objectives.

Sometimes, people may need to use formal processes and techniques, such as Brainstorming to develop ideas. You could also use a project or problem solving approach with structured steps and techniques to help a team focus on specific tasks or issues to work sequentially through to a new solution.

It is worth bearing in mind that creativity is a very individual process, so think through what techniques are likely to bring out the best results from the individuals in your team. For example, think about a structured approach that you would use to generate new, radical ideas from a team of extroverts. How would you modify this approach if you had a team of introverts?

Team Exercise: Discuss new ideas

Ask the team to discuss their performance in regard to the generation of new ideas.

Is the atmosphere and culture receptive to new ideas? Are processes and forums available to help ideas come forward? Are ideas encouraged? Does the team proactively share new ideas?

Use these questions to stimulate discussion and raise the team's awareness of creativity as a desirable team characteristic.

Agree as a team to consciously develop this aspect of the team's performance. Investigate what techniques you could use to do this and how they are used.

Use positive reinforcement to embed creativity in the team's culture. For example, present a "Bright Ideas" award either to the best idea each month or every time an idea that has the potential to create real impact is suggested. If your organisation already has its own award scheme, make soliciting nominations for this award a standing item on your monthly team meeting agenda.

Make the case for change

Effective teams focus on improvement. The team members are highly motivated to come up with new ideas all the time. External pressures can also force change upon the team at a rapid rate. With new ideas being presented all the time, teams need a way to evaluate which initiatives they should implement, and which ideas should receive approval for an allocation of funding and resources.

When new ideas are competing for funding and resources, you or the forums that approve the investment will want to evaluate each initiative using consistent criteria.

To do this, it is useful to have a standard template, which sets out:

- The idea - name and definition
- What will change as a result of the idea - impact on people, processes, risks and outputs
- The benefit the change will bring
- The cost and financial benefits
- Implementation considerations - timeframe, dependencies, level of complexity, resources required (internal and external)
- Which stakeholders are impacted? How are they impacted?

Keep these processes simple.

All change needs a 'business case' in order to gain sanction to proceed. In your team encourage the creation of the 'business case' mentality. It doesn't need extremely detailed processes for everything. Start with a little 'case' that takes a short time to prepare. Discuss the 'cases for change' each week with the team.

Develop the ones you want to take forward into larger more formal business cases in order to get approval to proceed and for funding and resources.

Keep a record of the team's business cases so recognition, learning and review can take place as ideas are implemented. Keep it simple and effective but keep it going!

Effectiveness Tips:

✓ Make creativity and innovation a priority

✓ Use processes and techniques to unleash creativity

✓ Use standard criteria to evaluate which new ideas to take forward and invest in

Effective Team Characteristic 18:
Has strong improvement mechanisms and processes

Teams have to tackle a multiplicity of problems and seize many opportunities. Sometimes a team is formed as a temporary measure just to tackle a particular issue.

Whether you lead or are part of a project team, a problem solving team or a permanent work team you will benefit from clear, structured tools and techniques to tackle problems and pursue opportunities.

Effective teams have structured approaches to implementing change and solving problems. These approaches improve the effectiveness and efficiency of these change processes and the management of their risks.

Without due process and the use of tools and techniques to manage change and improvement, the team is more likely to act in an ad-hoc, inconsistent and inefficient manner.

The use of structured approaches to change and problem solving also provides a great opportunity for individual growth. As individuals are exposed to these tools and techniques they will learn valuable skills that will serve them throughout their career.

There are many tools and techniques that govern change. Key processes include:

1. Problem solving

Often, problem solving requires a standardised approach and process that covers all of the key stages a team must go through to tackle root causes and develop sustainable solutions.

The focus is on implementing new ways of working that deliver improvements including reduced risk and costs.

There are various techniques on the market and one such technique can be found at **www.iWise2.com** called IMAGIINE[TM16].

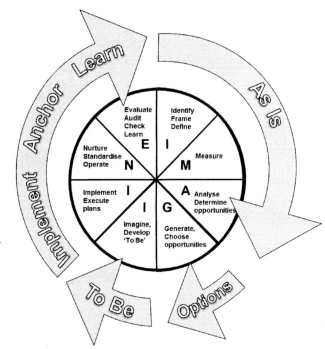

Figure 6 IMAGIINE[TM]

These techniques set out a number of steps to be followed in sequence to solve a problem. These frameworks will use a range of different tools and techniques within each step to assist you with the process.

2. Project or programme management

Projects and programmes critically require strong, comprehensive, measured and structured processes to facilitate effective delivery. These processes are critical because they will govern profound changes in processes, products and services. These programmes have risks, dependencies, resources, budgets and timeframes that need to be strictly managed in order to deliver the objective. They are often cross-functional, with the added complexity of managing many people from across the value chain including support functions.

Many companies have standard approaches that they require or encourage. Some have rigorous processes for controlling large projects and these include a series of milestones and gateways that permit a project to progress from one stage to the next. Interestingly, although these gateways are recognised as important, they are often not given the same credence for smaller projects within a team's own remit. It is useful to apply 'gateways' with defined 'go' or 'no go' criteria for any size of project.

Some approaches are proprietary and others, such as those used in Lean ⌊⌋ and Six Sigma ⌊⌋ environments are not. The most commonly used approach within a Lean or a Six Sigma environment is called DMAIC: Define, Measure, Analyse, Improve and Control. ⌊⌋

Figure 7 DMAIC

The five DMAIC steps provide a structured process to deliver a programme or project from the first stage of definition through to the implementation of on-going controls in the changed environment. DMAIC, like the problem solving approaches discussed earlier, uses different tools and techniques within each stage of the process.

Learning and using these techniques will bring a standard approach to addressing issues that follow all of the required steps to analyse the root cause of a problem rather than just the symptom.

To be able to use these techniques effectively requires training and education. Without this investment, people will learn as they go and will be less effective than they could be.

Team members who learn these techniques will be able to take that learning with them as they progress in their careers. By using the techniques in new situations they will build up a wealth of experience in how the techniques can be applied in practice.

Leader Exercise: Improvement competencies

Consider the techniques that your team members need to be proficient in to solve problems and effect change and improvement.

Assess team members' technical competency and consider whether they could apply these techniques more effectively if they had more classroom training or more experience.

Organise classroom training if this would be of benefit and consider any changes that you could make to leverage and improve experience levels within the team.

Effectiveness Tips:

✓ Use structured techniques and processes to implement change and solve problems effectively, efficiently and to manage risk

✓ Standard approaches focus on resolving root causes of problems, not just symptoms

✓ Improvement techniques require strong proficiency to be used effectively. Consider whether you need to enhance your or the team's knowledge with classroom training or more experience

Effective Team Characteristic 19:
Has clear decision making processes

One of the most challenging aspects of improving team performance is how to get the best decisions from the team.

As individuals we are often confident of our own decisions. We have rationalised them and we are convinced! There are also decisions we take when we believe we have no other option or when they are not unanimously approved or even when we are unsure but believe a decision has to be made. This also happens with team decisions however, a team's many voices and opinions increase the complexity of the process.

There are many dynamics that add to the complexity of team decision making. Some of these include varying:

- opinions
- data sets
- measurements
- levels of knowledge
- expertise

- experience
- willingness to voice an opinion, and
- levels of commitment to the outcome (with low levels of commitment possibly hidden from view)

A team needs to understand how it will take all of this into account and make effective decisions. This requires a process that hears and respects each view and then drives to a decision that the team supports. It also needs to facilitate timely decisions and ensure that in spite of dissenting views, everyone remains engaged and is supportive and committed to the decision and to the outcome.

Some decisions will be obvious; the leader will take others unilaterally. In other situations, a joint decision will be required and will need a high degree of engagement and support from the team.

As an important part of developing an effective team, you will need to decide as a leader to what extent you want to make the decisions yourself. Are you the type of leader that is 'it's my way or the highway?' Are you the type of leader that lets the team decide? Are you the type of leader who says 'I work on consensus', but the team really thinks that you are autocratic? Do you justify to yourself and others your decision making style or do you think that no justification is necessary?

Decision making is made more complex by the varying risk appetites of the individuals in the team. Some people are more comfortable with 'stretch' and ambiguity than others. Some are more comfortable with instant decisions. Some like to keep their options open until the last moment, or even keep raising the subject again and again even after the decision has been taken. As a leader, it is important to understand the risk appetites and preferences of your team members and manage the process so that it works for everyone.

Some leaders find handing over decision making to the team a threat and they fear a loss of control. It is interesting when these same leaders want more autonomy from their own boss, but don't see why their own team should have the same development opportunity. Getting this balance right is not easy. It needs careful consideration of what is best for each individual and each situation. The more that a team is involved in a decision, the higher their understanding, support, commitment and motivation to achieve the outcome will be.

Ultimately, various factors influence the degree of shared decision making and this should be understood and openly discussed with the team. Greater awareness of this is likely to increase team members' engagement.

Influences that affect the degree of shared decision making include:

The environment

The environment and culture of the organisation can influence individual leaders as they seek to follow role models or the perceived cultural 'way' in order to improve how they are perceived in the organisation.

The situation

In a situational leadership sense there are times when rapid 'taking command' and issuing 'directives' is clearly needed. The leader is carrying the prime leadership role, the power and the authority. This is often observed in a crisis. Sometimes however, the crisis is of the leader's own making, for example brought about by their own poor planning, structure, or lack of foresight. When this happens, a leader needs to focus on learning from mistakes and improving their planning and forecasting to help the team move forward and prevent such crises in future.

The members of the team

The maturity, stability, cohesiveness and competence of the team and its members will significantly influence their suitability for shared decision making. Moving away from being directive when the team is poorly skilled or unstable in some way may not be the best thing for the decision or for the business.

The leader's preferences and style

A leader has a certain style and this will impact their preference for making decisions. Some leaders are known for 'taking decisive decisions'; others have reputations for 'never making a decision'. The personality and decision making style of the leader will affect how the team performs and how the members feel.

Although there are range of decision making styles, it is usually advantageous to involve team members in the decision making process in order to benefit from the widest range of ideas, knowledge and experience. An effective team understands that this is not always possible, is aware of the range of decision making styles and knows what is the best to use in different situations.

Analyse the decision making styles at work in your team. How conscious is every one of the ways the team makes decisions and the advantages and disadvantages of each approach?

Use the Tannenbaum and Schmidt[17] Decision Making Continuum as a guide to the different levels of involvement and engagement that can occur in team decision making.

The diagram below is adapted from Tannenbaum and Schmidt's model:

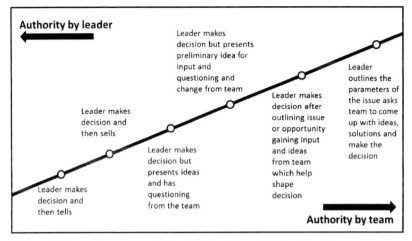

Figure 8 Tannenbaum and Schmidt Decision Making Continuum

Document Team Decisions

Have you ever been to an 'away day' that results in a big list of actions on a number of flip charts? Do you attend team meetings each week where there is a long action log, but you seem to be discussing what happened last week, again! Have you ever sat in a meeting that raised an issue again where you thought a decision had been taken at the last meeting? In fact your actions this week came about because of it!

Teams are often good at writing down actions and allocating responsibility for their completion. Experience shows they tend to be less good at documenting the decision.

This is strange because there can be a lot of time wasted by misunderstandings, actions that didn't seem to implement the decisions, different versions of the truth circulating and in the worst cases, confusion as people leave the meeting thinking different things have been agreed. If any of this sounds familiar to you, then the simple idea of documenting your decisions and confirming what has been agreed would be very valuable.

It is interesting to note what happens when leaders first try doing this. They are usually surprised by the feedback. They document a decision in language and in a manner they like and then send it out. They then are surprised by responses such as: 'I didn't see it quite like that' or 'that's not what we agreed' or 'it's been written from 'X' or 'Y's perspective, not mine'. These responses can be followed by a scream of protest when they see whom the decision has been communicated to. Why does this occur?

It often is the case that when we articulate an issue in a conversation with many inputs, it can be quite difficult to precisely summarise the outcome in language that everyone agrees with.

While not all decisions need to be documented, important decisions, which have wide ranging impact or are contentious, should be recorded. Documenting a decision and its rationale forms a very useful reference point and minimises the potential for people to waste time discussing an old issue again and again. It also helps people understand the context in which the decision was made and the influences acting on it at that time. When these conditions change, this understanding may signal that the decision needs to be revisited. Documenting the decision makes this possible, particularly if the original people involved have moved on.

Effectiveness Tips:

✓ Understand as a team how you will make decisions. This should include a process to consider a range of views yet drive to a decision that has the team's support

✓ Document key decisions and their rationale where they are important

Effective Team Characteristic 20:
Measures its performance, acts on facts not opinions

Effective teams are sure about one thing – how their performance and success is measured.

Without strong performance measures teams will not be able to track progress, and take corrective action if needed, towards their goals or assess customer satisfaction with the results.

The most important measures will assess the effectiveness of the team's:

- Alignment to the organisation's goals and strategies
- Outputs
- Processes
- Productivity and capability
- Competencies and skills
- Behaviours
- Progress on its development plans

It is essential that the team is clear on its objectives and how their success in delivering them will be evaluated.

This includes understanding why each measure that has been chosen is important and the priority of each, particularly from the perspective of stakeholders. If stakeholders use different measures to evaluate outputs, these also need to be understood.

Effective teams turn these measures into 'Key Performance Indicators' and use simple but clear scorecards to track their progress and to take action on underperformance as it arises.

Key points to note with regard to measurement:

1. Ensure that you have clarity on goals, objectives and targets
2. Ensure that you define and set your process measures so that you know whether you are delivering on your objectives and targets, and can identify and act on underperformance ·
3. Understand how to measure variation in process performance
4. Know how measurements are taken and that they are accurate
5. Know how to measure the capability of your processes i.e. their ability to deliver the required outputs
6. Use structured measurement techniques to measure performance, for example Control Charting, Run Charting and Capability Analysis.

Keep your measures simple but detailed enough to reflect the underlying performance. This is where skimming across the surface could miss the monster in the depths.

Regularly discuss with the team what the measures are and review the need for new measures, particularly when the business or processes change. Make sure that a strong base set of measures is set so that trends can be seen over time.

Team Exercise: Effectively measuring what is important

Examine each of your key deliverables.

- List the indicators that tell you that these deliverables are being achieved.

- How do these map to what you actually monitor?

- Does the frequency of each measure allow you to intervene in time to correct underperformance?

Effectiveness Tips:

✓ Ensure that you know how your performance and success is measured

✓ Define and set the key performance measures for your processes and outputs. Ensure that they enable you to monitor progress against objectives and targets and allow underperformance to be swiftly identified and acted on

✓ Know how your process measurements are taken and that they are accurate. Use structured measurement techniques to measure performance. Build and monitor trends over time

6 Behaviour

Team Effectiveness requires supportive behavioural norms. It requires strong trust, commitment and engagement.

The effective team rises to challenge and adversity and understands the emotional impact of change. It values diversity, communicates effectively and uses conflict constructively to drive better results.

The effective team understands how it influences perception in the rest of the organisation and gives recognition for behaviour and results that support Team Effectiveness.

It is results and action orientated while balancing the needs of the process, the team and individuals.

Behaviour is what is observable

Team behaviour and the behaviour of each individual in the team are of course critical to effectiveness and performance.

How the team works together and deploys its resources, skills, expertise and experience affects whether the team can move from an 'OK' to a 'great' team and then progress to an effective team. Counterproductive behaviours will derail these efforts.

One thing to keep at the forefront of your mind when working on behaviours as a means of improving effectiveness and performance is to focus on behaviour that is *observable*.

As the behaviour is observable, it is measurable and manageable. These characteristics distinguish actual behaviour from thoughts or intent.

Motivation, perception, culture, morale, climate, commitment and intentions are all important to understand, but in the end they combine and manifest themselves in observable behaviours.

The behaviour of the team is an integrated package of many influences.

As a leader, you will need to be clear with your team which behaviours you see as important. These should be written down and will be an input to any team building or development activity. Think about how you can use team development activities to create awareness of these behaviours, set expectations and agree actions to improve performance across the whole package.

This is not a superficial exercise. To gain real insight into what influences and drives observable behaviour, the team will have to dig into and be open about, root causes. Where behaviours are negative, the cause is likely to be highly sensitive.

Areas where the team is weak will require immediate attention as any negative or destructive behaviour may undermine or negate areas of strength. But don't forget your strengths. As well as addressing weaknesses, you should also spend some time understanding how your strengths work for you and how they are contributing to the team's effectiveness.

Effective Team Characteristic 21:
Delivers on its commitments and promises

An effective team meets its commitments.

Commitments are the foundations for delivery against detailed specifications and requirements. When performance standards are set, whether in the behaviour of the team or in the delivery of products or services, commitments are made.

Try using the words:

I commit to....

when defining outputs and deliverables with your customers or stakeholders.

Try using these words when discussing team norms and required behaviours. The phrase 'I commit' brings with it an emotional context. It brings in the heart as well as the mind. It brings in passion.

Some people find it hard to commit as they are unsure whether the deliverable can be achieved and so resort to 'I will try my best'. This is still a genuine response but pushing further to the 'I commit' statement will help bring out into the open any concerns and issues that are hindering the ability to commit.

Another technique to strengthen commitment is to turn deliverables into promises. Promises by their nature are very personal and carry strong emotional ties, which mean that most people find it more difficult to break a promise than an agreement or an objective.

Making promises to customers and colleagues can turn dry measurements into personalised service deliverables, bringing the emotion of the customers' needs into the task.

Try saying:

I promise to...

when agreeing to objectives or deliverables. Many people find this hard to do initially.

The reason that the 'commit' and 'promise' approach can be so powerful is that it forces the team to be open about any barriers to making a promise and any issues that prevent a commitment from being made. The team now has the opportunity to face up to, and try to resolve any problems that they think will impact their intended delivery at the outset, rather than leave them unsaid.

The worst thing a team can do is shrug their shoulders and see a person 'just not committing' instead of trying to really understand the root cause of the difficulty.

This is more of a problem when the person who is not committing has, for example, personal issues they don't want to discuss or cannot articulate a complex series of obstacles, the combination of which, they know, will cause problems. While these reasons for not committing will be legitimate for the person concerned, without this commitment, the team will be less effective.

When a firm commitment or promise is not forthcoming, work systematically using root cause analysis techniques to get to the real cause of the problem. This will help you tackle fundamental issues and not just symptoms.

A characteristic of an effective team is the belief that they can make these commitments and promises and stick to them. They become known for this characteristic. They become trusted to deliver. They get passed the ball because they will score.

Built on this belief is the agreement within the team to commit. This is a promise to deliver.

As a leader encourage goals and objectives to be stated as commitments and promises. Ensure that they are measurable.

Leaders Exercise: Turn objectives into commitments and promises

Examine your team's objectives. Consider how they could be expressed as promises or commitments. Test these out with the team. Solicit the responses 'I promise', 'We promise'.

Ensure that the root causes of any reluctance to promise or commit are systematically investigated and addressed.

Discuss with your team how it feels to have a set of 'promises'. What impact does this have on the team culture? On motivation? On engagement?

Discuss what it feels like when you fail to keep your promises.

Make your commitments specific and measurable and agree them with your key stakeholders. Convert your objectives into promises and commitments that can be measured to evaluate success.

Effectiveness Tips:

✓ Effective teams deliver on their commitments

✓ Turn objectives into commitments and promises that are measurable

✓ Document them as part of goal and objective setting

✓ Review achievement regularly

✓ Discuss barriers and enablers to keeping commitments and promises

Effective Team Characteristic 22:
Has strong trust

Trust is a vital component of an effective team.

It can be seen, for example, when team members actively support each other and don't have to chase one another for answers or inputs. Where there is a high degree of trust, the team works on the underlying assumption that things will be done and commitments will be delivered upon.

Trust in effective teams leads to feelings of loyalty and pride. The team members will often 'defend' the team and its members. This is both a good and a bad thing. Teams who drift into Groupthink and who only recruit people of like cultures will tend to trust each other. However, other aspects of this behaviour will not make them an effective team - even if they convince themselves that they are.

Trust is based on competence and character. Effective teams have a broad view that the team members are reliable, competent and are open to learning new skills and developing.

This trust leads to more disclosure and openness in communication and a strong belief that each individual will pull their weight. Where team members are given unfamiliar or stretching tasks, the other team members recognise this and provide encouragement and support.

Trust is important in relation to performance. If the team has made promises and commitments to achieving goals and objectives, these promises carry with them an implicit trust that they will be delivered. Trust is therefore integral to the concept of turning objectives into promises and the emotional commitment that they bring.

Leader Exercise: Trust and delivering on commitments

Think about your team and how it behaves. What aspects of the team's behaviour and processes can you observe that indicate that trust is present?

What part does trust play in the ability of the team to deliver on its promises and commitments?

How would a greater degree of trust:

- within the team
- between the team and its suppliers
- between the team and stakeholders

improve the effectiveness of the team's delivery?

Trust in Trust

Team norms are always present. All teams have them whether they are expressly defined or never discussed.

Effective teams maintain an awareness of their behaviour, commitments and promises.

It is difficult to overstate the impact of behaviour in the workplace. Indeed, many of our stresses at work are caused by other people's behaviour. Within the team context, an effective team works with and supports each other. Importantly, it also challenges each other in a way that is constructive and improves results.

Developing a code of behaviour as a reference point is a useful step. Again, the caution here is to make sure that the exercise is not just seen as a one off where the code gets hung on a wall and no one takes any notice of it! Whether the code hangs on the wall or not, what is important is that the team sets an expectation of, and then makes a commitment to, the norms and behaviours that it views as the most constructive.

Arguably, the single biggest influence on a team's behaviour is trust. It will determine how the team members relate to each other, the extent to which they are open and honest, share resources, rely on and support each other. It is critical when teams face a crisis and the members need to pull together.

The team's ultimate effectiveness will also, to a large degree be determined by trust. Trust in each other to play for the team as well as for themselves. Trust in the ability and competence of each member that they will bring these skills into play for the benefit of the team. Trust that they will support each other when things go wrong and when mistakes are made.

Trust is a sensitive subject. We all are trustworthy aren't we? However in relaxed moments by the coffee machine with our colleagues we can easily turn to '...I wouldn't trust them...' conversations.

As a leader, you need to know if there are trust issues in your team or indeed between yourself and team members. Trust, as the old adage says, is earned not demanded and a person's observed behaviour in the workplace demonstrates their trustworthiness. If you perceive that your team does not trust you, search for anything in your own behaviour that may have contributed to this. If there are trust issues between team members, you and or the parties involved will need to address the root causes if you want to continue to develop the team's overall effectiveness. Team building activities can also be used to build and strengthen trust.

If there is a lack of trust between your team and other units in the organisation, suppliers or other stakeholders, assess the potential impact that this could have on your ability to deliver. Consider what action you need to take to strengthen the relationship concerned.

Trust is characterised by a number of facets of behaviour that are grouped into trust in character and trust in competence. Writers such as Covey[18], Thomas and Schindler[19] all contribute to this thinking.

The diagram below is adapted from their ideas.

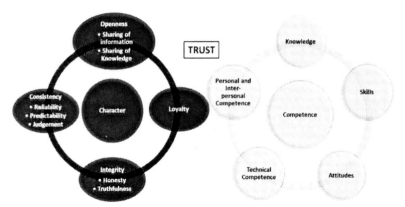

Figure 9 Trust Diagram, adapted from Covey, Thomas & Schindler

Effectiveness Tips:

✓ Understand the link between promises, commitment and trust

✓ Focus on trust as a key behaviour that will enhance or constrain your effectiveness

✓ Resolve any underlying causes of trust issues before trying to develop Team Effectiveness

Effective Team Characteristic 23:
Rises to adversity and challenge

How you react is so important

Things go wrong. Yes, I know we don't want to think that they will but they do. While we strive to minimise these occurrences and improve our performance, occasionally things do not go as planned.

When this happens leaders, teams, units, organisations, products, services, reputations and customer loyalty can be seriously affected by *how* the problem is dealt with.

There are many examples where promotions, products, services or technology have failed and customers have been let down. In some cases, the company responds poorly, further damaging customer confidence and significantly increasing the costs of the failure. In the worst cases, the company's mishandling of the situation does more damage to its reputation and its relationship with its customers, than the initial incident. In other cases, the company faces up to the incident quickly and engages with customers honestly and respectfully. This approach minimises the potential impact of the incident on reputation and costs and in extreme cases, when handled exceptionally well, can actually improve the organisation's image and reputation.

This equally applies to you and you team.

The most critical aspects for you and your team when something goes wrong are:

- Speed of recognition
- Speed of reaction
- Speed of communication

- Speed of action
- Understanding the context
- Understanding the criticality and importance
- Understanding the urgency
- Understanding the who, what, when, when and how
- Understanding what can be learned from the incident
- Understanding what needs to be done to rebuild confidence, relationships and trust with those who have been let down.

In order to learn and improve your behaviours and processes, when things go wrong analyse:

- The way the team recovers the situation and the processes that it uses to do this
- The resilience and robustness shown by the team after the situation to move forward and the processes that it uses to rebuild
- The demonstration of the above to the team members as well as other stakeholders
- How reactions improve.

Team Exercise: Improving reactions

Each quarter, review as a team any significant unexpected events:

- State how the event happened and its impact

- How did the team react and deal with the issue

- What was good about how the team reacted? Be specific

- What was not so good? Be specific. What impact did this have?

- What can be learned from this knowledge and experience?

- What needs to tangibly change to improve the way we react to issues? Who will do what to implement the change?

- Did we implement the changes that we decided at our last review?

- Have these changes resolved any issues in our previous reactions?

Effectiveness Tips:
- ✓ How you react is so important
- ✓ Be aware of how you are reacting to issues and assess your effectiveness
- ✓ Develop strategies that will help you respond rapidly and effectively to unexpected events. Have tested contingency plans in place where they are needed
- ✓ Be flexible. Adapt the way that you react to the needs of the situation and to incorporate learning from experience and feedback

Effective Team Characteristic 24:
Understands the emotional impact of change

It is important to know how people react and express their emotions as individuals and not stereotype potential reactions or assume that there is a 'group' response to change.

Things go wrong we know that. Trying to prevent problems and issues from occurring and doing things right first time is an essential aspect of team performance. However when things go wrong, a critical issue is how the team and the individuals within it respond.

When faced with a major issue or indeed a major change, we all go through phases of emotion. The news can startle us, it can shock us, while in some cases, it is just hard to believe.

When managing a team it is important to remember that when a big issue or change occurs, the team and each individual travel an emotional journey. Understanding this journey and recognising its symptoms and behaviours will allow the issue to be dealt with more effectively.

As well as travelling on an emotional journey, the team will feed off each other, looking for new norms and leadership. As the team does this, it is crucial to understand that every individual is moving at a different pace.

This is a difficult situation to manage as there is now more turbulence in the team than normal. Different behaviours emerge as each individual perceives different levels of pressure, challenge and stress. As team members begin to act differently the dynamics amongst them changes. The team may split into different sub-groups with similar feelings and emotions. This causes additional imbalances.

As this unfolds, recognition, strong leadership and a strong process are required to guide the team through the turbulence. The ability of a leader to recognise and respond to each individual's position, as well as the overall team status plus the needs of the task or situation will greatly assist the team's transition from the issue to a new future.

When faced with significant issues or change, we experience two pairs of opposing forces. These are illustrated in the diagram below.

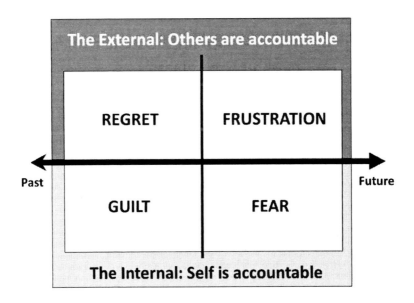

Figure 10 Forces of Change

In relation to the change, the two pairs of opposing forces are *our:*

1. perspective of the past and the future; and

2. view of who is accountable (others versus self)

The diagram shows a general view of the emotions created by the intersection of these forces. For example, a change imposed by others can result in regret, over the past that is lost, or frustration about the future. Of the four emotions, 'regret' and 'guilt' are the least likely to be able to allow an individual to move forward and accept the change. As a leader, this is very useful as you can focus your efforts on helping people who are demonstrating these emotions to progress.

In order to cope with change, we each go through an emotional journey[20] signified by the following phases, each attracting different behaviours and actions.

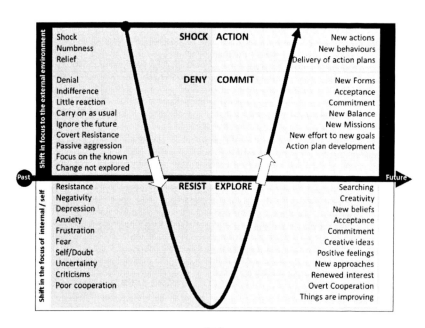

Figure 11 Emotional Change Journey

The diagram shows that when first faced with a change, we can experience a variety of emotions. These can range from feelings of relief and joy, through to shock and numbness.

This is often followed by a period of denial, which includes behaviours such as, carrying on as usual, not exploring the change or passive aggression. We then tend to move out of denial into a period of resistance, where uncertainty, anxiety, self-doubt and anger can cause negative behaviours. The length of time spent in these first three phases can vary significantly, during which, there is no movement towards accepting or building a new future.

In order to move forward, we need to travel through a period of exploration before committing to a new future and being proactive in creating it.

When you are implementing major change it is important that your project plans include actions to support this emotional journey.

When you are leading your people through change, ensure that you are aware of where they are on the emotional journey so that you can take the right actions to help them move to the next stage. For example, this may tell you when strong communication is needed to create certainty or that counselling and support is needed to help cope with shock. When people seem to be taking the news well and carrying on as normal, be careful that you do not assume that they have accepted the change, as they may be in denial.

The understanding that you show and the actions that you take as a leader to support the emotional change journey are important to move your team through instability and uncertainty to effectiveness. As part of your development as a team, learn to recognise these phases. Discuss them openly and support each other.

Leader Exercise: The emotional journey

Examine behaviours that you are seeing in relation to a current significant change impacting your team.

What do these behaviours tell you about how people are coping and progressing through the change?

What can you do differently to help the change process and support the people in it?

Effectiveness Tips:

✓ Change involves an emotional journey. Understand this journey and support your team and each individual through it

✓ Use the diagrams as a useful guide to help understand what is happening in the team in times of change and provide support

✓ Examine how the team and each individual is coping with change and plan effective actions to help move the team along the journey to a new future

Effective Team Characteristic 25:
Uses conflict constructively

We have all experienced teams where the internal wrangling for time, money, expertise and effort produces conflict and many opinions. Faced with tight time constraints and seemingly endless new demands, the team can struggle to allocate their resources effectively and efficiently to all tasks and deliverables.

These conflicts can create stress for team members and lead to relationship conflicts.

As a leader, you need to understand the types of conflict and judge how best to manage conflict so that it is constructive and contributes to team's overall results and development.

An effective team should aim for:

- Low interpersonal and relationship based conflict
- Intermediate levels of task conflict, depending on the criticality of the tasks and deadlines
- Low levels of process conflict

As we are all human the potential for conflict is always present. Indeed, a team with no conflict will most likely be underperforming, due to potential Groupthink, conformity enforced as a norm, or a culture of 'yes men.' A degree of conflict is to be expected if your team uses healthy challenge as a means of constantly questioning and driving improvements in performance.

Work with your team to set ground rules for dealing with conflict. Ensure that mutual respect and understanding for other people's perspectives, as well as structured processes for getting to solutions are adopted.

Remember that some types and levels of conflict can assist in the quality of questioning and challenge, but others can seriously derail the team. The team leader needs to constantly manage and be alert to the balance of stresses inside the team to ensure optimal performance, engagement and the on-going development of the team and the individuals within it.

Don't be conflicted by conflict

Some see conflict as good within a team. Some see it as bad.

This probably reflects each individual's own nature and working style, for example, whether they are aggressive or assertive, whether they welcome ideas or enjoy telling and directing rather than collaboration. Can you name people that you think enjoy aggression? Do they really help the organisation or unit? Is it the type of conflict that helps team performance or not?

Conflict can take many forms in a team environment. The most debilitating is where individuals are in direct conflict with each other. This may be because of a clash of personality or some perceived or actual issue. Direct relationship conflict can be extremely stressful and often makes it impossible to think clearly and objectively about the role, the tasks and the objectives. In some cases, this stress can be all consuming and can lead to people leaving the organisation. People have different ways of dealing with these situations from becoming more aggressive, to completely withdrawing. Communication usually becomes strained or people avoid talking to each other altogether.

As a leader, it is vital that you recognise quickly if this situation begins to develop or is present. It will directly reduce the team's effectiveness. People will not be focused on the information and decisions they need to make - they will be distracted and will not be actively listening to what is going on around them.

In addition, they may begin to automatically reject ideas and information from the person that they are in conflict with.

Don't ignore this situation and don't wait to act. Work with the individuals to help resolve the issue before it debilitates them and the team. It is particularly important not to try and deal with this in the open team environment but to work with the individuals outside of team forums.

Although relationship conflicts are debilitating, conflicts about ideas, activities and tasks can either be a positive or a negative force.

Where conflict focuses on facts, strategies plans, ideas and decisions without getting personal, it is more likely that the process will be constructive. Conflicting ideas can be expressed and discussed openly, even vigorously without causing offence and as a result, this approach is more likely to generate better ideas, solutions and decisions.

While conflict can generate new ideas for improvement and help creativity, in some cases it can be negative and no consensus or way forward results.

Conflict can also arise in teams over perceived simplicity and complexity of tasks. For example, where one group has competence in an area they can view a task as simple and just want to get on with it. Others who do not have the competence may see the tasks as complex. If the experts are held back from taking action, this will create frustration and conflict that can slow the team down.

On the reverse side, when tasks are complex or the future is unclear or no one knows the answer, many competencies may need to be drawn together.

In this case, conflict and creativity can go hand in hand and be seen as a positive force that does not dissatisfy those involved. This type of conflict can assist a group get to the root cause of an issue, implement change more successfully and avoid Groupthink.

Some other common sources of conflict within a team are the allocation of roles and responsibilities, the allocation of resources and competition for team resources.

Leader Exercise: Conflict

Assess your handling of a recent team conflict and how you can improve your conflict management skills.

- Take a recent conflict within the team or between the team and another party. Define the conflict specifically

- Identify what, in your view, caused the conflict

- What happened during the conflict?

- What was the result of the conflict?

- What was the outcome after the conflict and with the passage of time?

- What was done well? What was done poorly?

- What are the key lessons?

Effectiveness Tips:

✓ Use conflict constructively – a range of opinions and healthy debate generates better quality ideas, solutions, decisions and facilitates continuous improvement

✓ Be quick to identify and resolve debilitating conflict

Effective Team Characteristic 26:
Has strong feelings of engagement

Engagement is an increasingly used term these days. Many organisations use engagement surveys as a measure of 'people' or 'human resources' performance.

Engagement revolves around concepts of the employee being involved in the business, their emotional attachment to their job, team and organisation and the amount of discretionary effort they give. It is tied to the concept of energising employees and creating conditions where they naturally 'go that extra mile'.

High levels of employee engagement have been linked in studies to high organisational performance. High employee engagement is also linked to high commitment and productivity.

The behaviours of engaged employees will include being proactive, having high energy levels, wanting to give more and looking for solutions rather than hiding behind issues.

Many aspects of developing Team Effectiveness will deliver higher levels of engagement. These include knowing what is expected through role and goal clarity, being able to use skills and talents effectively and having opportunities to learn and develop. If a person feels able to contribute to the workings of the team and have a say, is involved in decision making and is recognised for good work, both effectiveness and engagement benefit.

One of the important aspects of engagement is to what degree a person feels they can affect the products, services and deliverables of the team. Overarching these is the concern that an organisation has for its employees' health and wellbeing.

As a leader, detecting disengaged employees is important, as it will help identify issues that are affecting Team Effectiveness and the well being of the individual.

Observing behaviours that indicate that an employee is disengaged is the first step. Disengaged behaviours will be a symptom of some deeper underlying root cause that is likely to be impairing effectiveness.

People in effective teams feel engaged. They often feel that everyone in the team is engaged, contributing, involved and that no one is isolated or left out.

This will even be the case when things are not going well for the team. This sense of inclusion and engagement helps build the basis for trust and teamwork.

Engagement is now receiving a lot of attention as a key measure of employee performance. If your organisation does not conduct a formal engagement survey, consider developing a questionnaire that examines employee engagement and aims to highlight opportunities for improvement.

Make engagement one of your team's primary measures.

Talents and team energy

It is interesting to look back as a team leader at the teams that you have been involved in to learn lessons from the past. List the primary teams you have been part of over the last number of years. Now look at the makeup of those teams and how the competencies and experience within the team were used.

Many people who have been part of a high performing team often point to high utilisation of the competencies in the team. People describe the experience as one where people seemed to give 110% effort and everyone's skills were put to great use. They were motivated by being able to do what they do best and work with others who were also playing to their strengths.

A team where the individuals are able to perform at their best creates a buzz, a tangible group energy and the conditions for high achievement. This combination of ideas, skills and energy creates a level of achievement far greater than any individual effort could achieve.

Members of high performing teams often speak about how the environment was challenging, stretching and sometimes seemingly impossible. Alongside this, they describe breaking through to new ideas, new levels, achieving things that they didn't think were possible. They express surprise at what they achieved as a team.

The effort temperature was high. The sense of challenge was high. The sense of involvement, engagement, contribution and achievement was high.

This level of stimulation and challenge can be exhausting but the feeling of achievement is long standing and deep.

High performing teams rise to challenges in spite of difficulties and obstacles. When each member can contribute their talents and the best that they have to offer to the task and to the team, high levels of energy, motivation, achievement and satisfaction result.

Learn how you can make maximum use of the talents and strengths in your team. Make a point of monitoring the team's energy level and consider whether improving your use of talent can raise it.

Effectiveness Tips:

✓ Effective teams are engaged

✓ People enjoy doing what they do best and are highly motivated and energised by contributing to the team in this way

✓ Assess whether you are making the best use of the combined talents and abilities in your team

Leader Exercise: Talents and team energy

Assess how you leverage the talent in your team and team energy levels.

- Are you using all of your people to the best effect? What talents and capabilities in the team can you make better use of?

- Are your team members challenged to achieve a new level of performance and stimulated to solve issues and problems?

- Do they face these with realism, strength of conviction and commitment?

- How do the team members describe belonging to this team?

- What do team members feel about this team?

- What do you feel about this team and its effort?

- Is there a healthy level of challenge within the team?

- What should change?

- Project forward and place yourself a year in the future. Now look back, how will you describe this team experience?

From all these findings, how would you describe the team's energy levels?

What can you observe as 'energy indicators' so that you can take the team's 'energy temperature' from time to time and after any actions that you have taken to improve it?

Effective Team Characteristic 27:
Values diversity and uses it to its advantage

Two of the death knells for teams is Groupthink and recruiting like, which can result in stale, uniform thinking. While debate and challenge may be taking place, a team's limited diversity will mean that they are not as creative and as effective at generating new thinking, ideas and solutions as they could be.

Many leaders can easily slip into recruiting people 'like them', people they 'like' or at worst, 'yes men'. Managing and leading diverse teams with a wide range of backgrounds, experiences, expertise and thinking is much harder than managing teams that are not diverse. As a result, many shy away from this challenge under the guise of 'cultural fit'.

Senior teams with diverse experience, background, capabilities and competencies have been shown to demonstrate better innovation and decision making.

While recruiting people from diverse backgrounds brings the potential for better decisions and performance, it does not do the trick on its own. The team needs processes that allow the members to learn from each other and the situations they face and encourage open and honest discussion, sharing and dialogue. These processes should be aimed at generating new ideas and solutions and make good use of strong questioning and critique. They should also facilitate the bonding of the team and strong teamwork.

Teams that can achieve this and who are able to recognise the contribution and perspective of each member, have the potential to work together to achieve far more as a team than they can by working as individuals.

Effective teams use diversity – but watch for splinters

Building highly effective teams is not easy. Building from a base of diverse experience and skills makes the challenge harder.

Team development is a journey, and there is no magic wand that turns an immature team or group into an effective team in an instant.

If you take the more challenging, but more rewarding path of recruiting and developing diversity in your team, you will travel a harder pathway. On this pathway, there will be times when your team is diverse, and other times when it lacks diversity. A team that is in the middle of the diversity scale needs special care, as it is vulnerable to the adoption of some negative behaviour when faced with difficult times or challenges.

These behaviours generally involve splinter groups appearing in the main team structure. These splinter groups occur for example, when a faction feels threatened against the rest or sees opportunities, which it wants to grasp not being taken. In these circumstances, corridor conversations start occurring and splits begin to appear. Individuals club together for strength and protection for fear of isolation.

It is very important to detect the first signs of this activity and use team building and development activity to bring the team together and strengthen relationships.

The power of personalities

We are all different. That is the joy of a team. Different skills, attitudes, knowledge, experience and education. Different needs, wants and aspirations. This is what makes a team so powerful, yet so difficult to manage to achieve high performance.

A team is made up of individuals, each with their own personality. An effective team whilst developing powerful norms and cohesive behaviours uses the power of each individual within it. It will not seek to clone a particular person or approach but will set examples and best practice and will provide a variety of different role models.

As you get to know your people, you will get to know their personalities. Try to understand what makes them tick.

Understanding more about a person's personality and personal preferences helps you build rapport. Whilst this kind of approach is not the be all and end all of working with team members, it does provide a strong foundation for working together.

Personality is an enduring set of characteristics that help explain a person's behaviour. Since we are focusing on the impact of behaviour on team and individual performance, spending time understanding personalities is a very helpful part of this process.

There are a number of approaches to the study of personality ranging from studies of traits through to the belief in 'self'. Some of the most popular look at indicators built from the work of Carl Jung.[21] One of the most well-known and widely used approaches is the Myers-Briggs[22] Type Indicator.®

Jung's foundation and Myers-Briggs' work looks at personality in a number of dimensions:

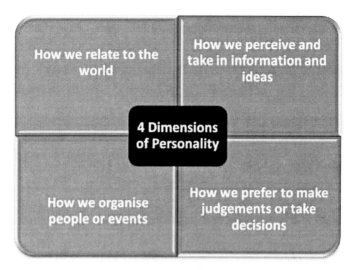

Figure 12 Myers-Briggs Type Indicator®

Use analysis like Myers-Briggs' to develop an understanding amongst the team of different personality preferences. Use this insight as a platform for discussion.

Whilst tools like this have their supporters and detractors, personality does affect behaviour and performance. In a team situation, the dynamic created by each personality can have a positive or negative effect on team's overall performance and cohesion. Improving the team's awareness of how each member's personality influences the team dynamic is therefore a valuable step in building effectiveness.

Raising awareness of the influence of personality on team performance by discussing individual preferences and styles is one way of developing a team's overall effectiveness. From this analysis, the team can develop processes and ways of working, which recognise and respect the uniqueness of each individual and use their preferences to the team's advantage.

This helps the team to learn from each other and improve communication and decision making.

Effectiveness Tips:

- ✓ Diverse teams expand the team's experience and viewpoints, increasing the potential for better questions, ideas, solutions and decisions
- ✓ Watch for splinters
- ✓ Understanding personalities is the first step in understanding behaviour and each team member's influence on the team dynamic
- ✓ Improving your understanding of preferences can improve the impact of your communication, recognition, learning and coaching processes

Effective Team Characteristic 28: Communicates and shares openly and honestly

Undiscussables

What is taboo in your team? Anything? What is not discussed or not encouraged?

All teams and groups can suffer from either temporary or permanent issues that are not discussed and appear to be signalled as 'off the agenda.'

In some cases it is because the organisation or the leader signals no appetite for the subject. Sometimes the subject is very sensitive. Sometimes individuals perceive it to be the best interests of others to not discuss it. Sometimes there is history.

Some undisscussables such as gossip, while unhelpful, are irrelevant to the functioning of the business. Some are not. They cause tension and distraction, feeding rumours and potentially clouding decision making. The team needs to work through these issues and resolve them so that they can move forward.

In many cases ironically, these tend to be the secrets that everyone already knows. It is remarkable how the grapevine and gossip machine works. Some would argue that as human beings this aspect of socialisation and interaction is needed. Whatever the case, it is incredible how fast information moves - when it is finally 'officially' released, there are many nodding heads who are 'already in the know'.

Of course in some business situations, such as sensitive projects, mergers, takeovers and other negotiations confidentiality is paramount. However, a team that can disclose more and be open about issues has more of a chance to bind, benefit from a healthy exchange of information that creates reassurance and certainty, and move forward.

There will be a natural degree of trepidation around raising sensitive subjects or information that is not yet supposed to be widely known. Some will know information and be unsure whether it should be aired in a certain way. Some will know information and deliberately hold it back. Again, while secrecy sometimes is required, when the team can be open about issues that are fuelling rumours, uncertainty and inhibiting performance safely, they will build greater trust and deeper cooperation.

The key here is safe. What is said in the room stays in the room. A safe environment allows more public disquiet to be aired and allows people to express a whole range of emotions and engage in questioning that would otherwise be suppressed.

Safe is easy to say but as these are the sensitive or taboo subjects it is not easy to achieve. It also relies on the trust the team members have in each other. It is not good if nine out of ten team members observe the need to keep an issue within the team and one does not. As soon as they tell one other person, before you know it, the whole world seems to know.

Codes and charters of behaviour that permit team members to bring undiscussables out into the open, coupled with the provision of safe mechanisms and processes for that discussion, will facilitate greater team development and effectiveness.

At the highest level, companies provide mechanisms like whistle blowing policies and procedures or even employ outside investigators and auditors to uncover issues. These processes may or may not be at work in your organisation. However, this does not take away the need to develop a culture, a climate and an atmosphere that permits the discussion of challenging issues that inhibit openness, productivity and the progress of the team.

Remember 'safety' is key here as if fear exists people will be far less willing to open up.

Sharing

Sharing is one of the immediate and obvious characteristics of an effective team.

Sharing comes in many forms:

- Data
- Information
- Knowledge
- Wisdom
- Experience
- Communication
- Tasks
- Activities
- Skills

In effective teams, one thing that stands out is the natural willingness and vibrancy of sharing. Team members want to share and learn from others. A vibrant sharing culture within a team helps all team members:

- Grow and develop
- Learn
- Build bonds
- Tackle tasks more effectively
- Tackle tasks more efficiently

Most people agree that sharing is a positive feature although some only see the need to do this when they think that it is appropriate. In some circumstances this works as each individual is contributing their expertise and letting others do the same. However in others, withholding information can inhibit the speed at which a team can move, make decisions and develop.

The barrier often encountered in this area of Team Effectiveness is the perception by some that knowledge is power. This is of course in many situations, true, but an effective team is willing to forgo this in exchange for the greater benefit that more disclosure has on the team's development and performance.

Sharing can challenge individuals particularly those who like to keep their thoughts to themselves. As a leader, be aware of different personalities and their natural traits. Some will act in an extroverted manner, while others will offer suggestions after a period of reflection. Be careful as a leader that you do not have a 'right' way that imposes on the personality of others.

When teams are effective, sharing is natural and a reflection of goodwill, camaraderie and a desire to help each other achieve desired outcomes.

Think about the extent to which your team naturally shares. Is there anything that you can do to create an environment in which people would be more sharing?

Test this out.

If you feel that the team is not sharing naturally or seems to have reservations about sharing, this may reflect personality traits or habit. However, a reluctance to share could be a sign of a deeper issue in the team such as conflict or a lack of trust. Perhaps there is fear in the team about what will happen if information is shared.

For example does one person 'steal' ideas and present them as their own? Or maybe one person does not trust another or has a perception that they cannot contribute to the current problem sufficiently.

Or perhaps the organisation's reward mechanisms are so individual centric that keeping ideas to oneself is the best way to get ahead. Whilst an individual generating the ideas must be rewarded, an element of great team working is using these ideas to help others in the team without the person who came up with the idea feeling threatened.

As a leader, raising the issue of sharing and wanting more of it can sometimes been seen as a false forcing of a behaviour or even threatening. If sharing is not as proactive and as strong as it could be, sensitively investigate and take action on the root causes. Use team building as a means of strengthening trust and relationships.

Leader Exercise: Sharing self-assessment

Take the temperature of sharing in your team by rating the team against the following:

- My team is good at sharing

- My team has good processes to facilitate sharing

- Sharing occurs naturally in my team

- We discuss opportunities to share more

- I am satisfied that the level of sharing taking place is making my team effective

- I am clear about any barriers to sharing and ways to encourage greater sharing

---

Use these questions to develop a temperature check as part of your own analysis of the team's performance. Do this consistently over a few quarters to check progress and use it as the basis for investigating root causes of any reluctance to share.

Effectiveness Tips:

✓ Create an environment that encourages the constructive airing of the 'undiscussable'

✓ Great teamwork is typified by natural, proactive sharing

✓ If sharing does not flow naturally, look for deeper causes, as they are also likely to be limiting Team Effectiveness in a number of ways

Effective Team Characteristic 29: Makes Meetings Work

Team meetings are an important part of the functioning of any team. They provide a key opportunity for team members to interact, share information, report and gain clarity of performance need and direction.

Types of Team Meeting

Team meetings take many forms and have morphed into a series of variations each with their own name. Examples of this are: Team Briefings, Stand Up Meetings, Team Talks and Team Huddles.

Time allocated

Team meetings have a variety of lengths and venue arrangements depending on their particular objectives and availability of personnel. These meetings have grown from the obvious gathering of everyone in one place to extensive use of conference calls, webinars, virtual class or meeting rooms and video conferencing.

Some people seem to spend their life in meetings and find it very hard to find time outside these meetings to 'get things done'.

Importance

Team leaders on the whole see Team Meetings as critical for the leadership, development and focus of the team week by week.

Satisfaction

Most leaders appear to understand the simplicity of needing meetings and are generally aware that there are various ways in which they could conduct them. Yet, a lot of team members have the view that Team Meetings are 'a waste of time', 'could be done in half the time', 'prevent them getting on with the job', 'don't let their voice be heard' or are 'just a one way transmission of information'.

It is even worse is when these sentiments are held at senior levels and senior personnel spend time secretly checking their smart phone, emails or texting when they feel no one is watching. These behaviours demonstrate the inability of Team Meetings to meet the collective needs of the team members and lead to behaviours that disrespect the whole and whoever is speaking.

This demonstrates that many leaders still have opportunities to make their meetings more effective.

Basics

Team meetings can consume vast amounts of valuable time and money. It is important to use these sessions effectively.

The basics of a good Team Meeting are, reasonably basic, yet it is surprising how often they are not executed in a way that meet the needs of the team, the individual members and the organisation. The basic needs of a Team Meeting are that:

1. It is planned. This means planned for a success with a constructive agenda, not just planned in the diary.

2. It involves all of the team and does not leave certain members out, leading to feelings of being overlooked and excluded

3. It has clear leadership of each section of an agenda.

4. It has enough time for each item.

5. Timing is provided in advance so that people know how much time they have, so they can tailor presentations and material.

6. It allows enough time for discussion.

7. Materials are issued in advance. In advance not meaning 30 seconds before the meeting starts, allowing no one any chance of reading the material or understanding it.

8. It has a clearly signalled purpose behind each item so that people are prepared to either hear information, receive presentations or make decisions.

These basics will obvious to most people. However the source of much discontent lies in the failure to execute them. Think about the last few meetings that you have attended. Are the basics well executed or does material arrive at the last minute? Does the meeting constantly overrun on agenda item 1 leaving the last agenda items (that may have been important to you), rushed or postponed?

Reinforce and instil the discipline of these basics in your team. If you see negative behaviours like those described above, your meetings are not as effective as they could be.

Getting the agenda right
Time each item appropriately. In addition, signal whether each item is:

I for **Information:** communication only to the team members with assimilation and action required as instructed by the communication

C for **Consultation:** communication designed to consult team members. While the team members will not be the final arbiter or decision-maker, they are being consulted on the issue in question

D for **Decision:** a clear signal that a decision will be taken at this meeting. This signals to attendees that decision-makers need to be present

DI for **Discussion**: the expectation is that no decision will be required but the time will be used to raise an issue and gather thoughts and opinions as input to further consideration

These are just examples and many leaders have developed their own way of signalling what is expected. This not only helps the team members prepare for the meeting but also helps the person organising the agenda to structure each item so that it meets an objective.

Making the meeting work

The type of meeting, the available time, location of the people and the content all dictate the time, location and structure of the meeting.

Team member input and satisfaction are important elements to making meetings work and should be monitored. Most people want an effective meeting so proactively ask for improvement ideas. Always ask your team members if the meeting is working and discuss as a team, how it could be improved and made more effective for them.

To meet or not to meet that is the question

Meetings do need to be held. However, much can be achieved without them. Be sure that you are not just having them for meetings' sake. On the flip side, watch out for managers that avoid having meetings and provide no opportunity for the team to discuss or question actions and decisions together.

Making the whole thing work

A checklist for effective meetings:

1. Don't have a meeting in the first place if the issue can be addressed another way

2. Have full attendance for the whole meeting when it is required and don't when it is not

3. Avoid attending all of a meeting where you don't contribute to 90% of it. Discuss this with the leader and work out whether you need to be there for governance, information or contribution or whether you can drop in or out, or delegate attendance

4. Always set clear objectives for the meeting

5. Distribute agendas in advance, clearly signalling the intent and time required for each item

6. Prepare, and ensure that all attendees are prepared. Circulate any pre-reading and other documents for the meeting in advance

7. Time the meeting appropriately and give enough warning of its scheduling. Start and finish on time

8. Give time for people to get from one meeting to the next

9. Make sure that everyone understands the priorities of the meeting and each agenda item

10. Stick to the agenda

11. Record the actions and the key decisions. Circulate these to combat the comment later 'that's not what I remember agreeing'

12. Summarise decisions and agreements at the end of the meeting and in all circulated documents

13. Cultivate positive behaviours that that make the meeting effective. Watch for, and discourage negative behaviours such as leaving the room, taking calls, emailing, texting and side conversations

14. Follow up actions. Have a robust process to ensure that this is done

15. Give positive reinforcement and recognition of effort and results

16. Continuously assess the effectiveness of your meetings and use feedback and input from the team to keep improving.

Team Exercise: Effective meetings

Review the functioning of your team meetings. Assess them against the basics.

- What can be improved in terms of behaviour?

- What can be improved in terms of structure and process?

- What commitments can the team make to improve the meetings?

- How will the team monitor its improvements?

- How will the team and leader recognise good team behaviours and process?

- How can we make team meetings work for us?

Effectiveness tips:

✓ As a team, know and deliver the basics of effective meetings

✓ As a team, monitor behaviours and performance

✓ Only hold meetings when they are needed

✓ Regularly assess the effectiveness of team meetings

✓ Maintain focus on continuous improvement and use feedback and input from the team to facilitate this

Effective Team Characteristic 30: Respects communication preferences

It is obvious that communication is key to a team or any other set of human relationships. Yet, communication can easily top the list of reasons for employee dissatisfaction.

Today there are so many ways to communicate and as we all have our communication sending and receiving preferences, it can be difficult to get it right.

And there is so much communication. It's not uncommon for a person to receive so many incoming emails that they would have to spend every minute of their day responding if they dealt comprehensively with every one of them. With text, chat, Twitter, Blogs, LinkedIn, Facebook and other social networking sites, the ability for us to communicate rapidly continues to grow. Keeping pace with all of this can be challenging.

With so many inputs and feeds we can quickly be sucked in to a 'Headline' culture, which sees us skimming the surface of many topics. In one sense, that is not a bad thing as we cover a vast array of different information and opinions, which produces a broader input base. However the pace and volume of incoming communications, options and opinions can make it difficult for us to penetrate more deeply into a subject.

In order for you to communicate effectively, an important factor to consider is the form of your communication. People tend to have preferences and these may vary in certain situations. Some are frustrated by email and respond better to a phone call. However, if someone is in meetings all day, text message or electronic communication might be best, although they may not prefer it.

Effective teams are aware of these preferences and agree how they will communicate and how long they will take to respond. Where a situation requires on-going communication, they will agree the frequency and the format that this will take. Whilst these protocols cannot stop the natural flow of everyone talking to everyone else and nor should they, formally agreeing what is appropriate and what works helps oil the flow of communication and hence effectiveness.

Effective teams ensure that they have a well thought out process for communicating to the wider organisation. They will carefully consider how best to promote their activity in the organisation and will consciously influence and manage how they communicate to formal forums in the business and to stakeholders. In this way, the team ensures that stakeholders receive consistent messages, in order to maintain their confidence and support. The team will carefully adapt the content, format and frequency of the communication to each situation so that it best supports their aims.

Effective teams also measure how well they communicate externally and seek feedback in order to continuously refine this aspect of their performance.

Leader Exercise: Managing stakeholder communication

- List all of your stakeholders and check that you have a communication objective for each.

- Have you set out a communication plan that meets each objective?

- If your team communicates with a stakeholder on a number of levels (for example, at a leadership, and separately at a working level), is there a co-ordinated communication objective and plan for each?

- What is your process to request feedback on how effectively your communication meets your stakeholders' needs for information?

- How is this feedback used to refine the way that you communicate?

- Discuss this with your team to ensure that everyone shares a common view and commits to communicate with stakeholders only in the agreed manner.

	Team Communication Checklist	
1.	Who do we need to communicate to within the team - is it understood?	
2.	Who do we need to communicate to outside of the team - is it understood?	
3.	Have we identified our prime communications?	
4.	Have we prioritised our prime communications?	
5.	Are we clear on the presentation, format and frequency of our prime communications?	
6.	What feedback do we have on how well our communications meet stakeholder needs?	
7.	Do we have a process to gather feedback and use it to refine our communications?	
8.	Do we have a process to understand how we all feel about the way that we communicate?	
9.	How do we know how others feel about the way that we communicate?	
10.	Are our communications open and honest?	
11.	What results do we expect from our communications?	
12.	Do we understand each other's communication style and how it helps us?	
13.	Are we clear when special communication focus and effort is needed?	
14.	Are we balanced between in-team and extra-team communications?	

Communication types and direction

There are several key communication types and directions that are important for the team to know and to consciously use.

It is easy to allow tasks, deadlines, time constraints and general complacency to get in the way of the team giving appropriate attention and priority to these communication types. As a consequence, team communication can get out of balance and this can quickly lead to dissatisfaction for team members and stakeholders. The team leader and or the team members may not even be able to pin point a tangible reason for emerging feelings of dissatisfaction.

These communication types are:

Task and Transactional Communication

This involves either one-way or two-way communication around the tasks, information and processes that the team needs in order to function. It typically covers demands, performance needs, outputs and outcomes and can range from specific detail to high level overviews. It can require written support material and presentation methods.

Relationship Communication

This is communication used by team members to build understanding of each other, what they feel and what they think. It is often exploratory and frequently unsupported by written material. By definition it is primarily a two-way exercise and likely to be in person. The emphasis is on building a cohesive unit and trust amongst the team members or with others outside of the team.

These two basic types of communication must be in balance for the team to function effectively. Ensure that in your team that you do not favour one to the detriment of the other, for example, focusing so much on tasks and deliverables that relationship and other needs are neglected.

Intra-Team

Together, transactional and relationship communication are used within the team and help the team operate effectively and develop as a cohesive unit. An effective team challenges itself on how it operates and seeks to avoid Groupthink and complacency. The balance of communication should be designed to support the team achieve these aims.

Extra-Team

Both transactional and relationship communication are needed for the team to operate effectively with other teams, groups, forums and stakeholders. Teams need to focus sufficient attention on both their internal communication needs as well as on external communication that confirms their organisational fit and builds effective relationships.

A particularly effective tool for extra-team communication is the RACI (Responsible, Accountable, Consulted and Informed) matrix. This involves agreeing and documenting who is accountable and who is responsible for each action or deliverable. These parties should agree their accountability and responsibility and commit to these roles. Any parties that need to be consulted and informed are also agreed and documented.

To ensure that their extra-team communication is effective, teams should examine how they:

- decide who will be consulted in decisions and actions. This requires an effective process to facilitate the consultation, including requesting feedback.

- decide who will be informed about performance, decisions and actions but will not be consulted on the performance or approach. This requires a different communication approach, as the team has already decided on the action.

- provide progress updates. Includes both formal and informal updates to keep relevant parties up to date so that there are no shocks or surprises.

- explore. Going to other environments and teams in order to learn and bring back information that the team can use to improve its performance and help its development.

- promote the performance of the team, either formally or informally.

Communication Direction: The external compass

Communication can go in many directions. Some intended some not. Be clear about the directions that you need to communicate in, in order to successfully manage your stakeholders.

Onwards and upwards - true north

Teams must manage their relationships and performance with the organisation's senior leadership and their associated teams. The effectiveness of this communication will influence the perception those leaders and teams have of the team's performance and its members.

East to West

This is communication across the team's value chain with suppliers, enablers and customers.

It aims to improve the way teams and individuals work together and the performance of the end to end processes along the value chain.

The spinning needle

This approach is to spin around the 'world-outside', including competitors, markets, the environment and the industry. This communication process scans the broader world that affects the team, creating an awareness of the team or organisation in the broader external environment.

Leader Exercise: Communication types and direction

- Consider each communication type and direction. Assess how effectively you use each and maintain the right balance across them.

- Do you have clear communication objectives? Is your communication planned and executed in order to achieve these?

- Use The Communication Matrix below to map your key communications. Assess the balance of your effort, time and success. Discuss communication with your team and how it could be improved.

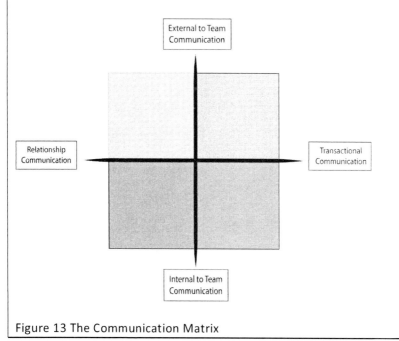

Figure 13 The Communication Matrix

Effectiveness Tips:

✓ Be aware of communication preferences

✓ Agree team communication formats, methods, frequency and response times

✓ Know your stakeholders' communication needs and preferences

✓ Have a communication objective and plan for each stakeholder

✓ Actively seek feedback and use it to refine your communication's effectiveness

✓ Carefully plan stakeholder communications, keep messages consistent

✓ Balance transactional and relationship communications, both within the team and with external parties

✓ Evaluate how you decide which external parties need to be consulted, informed and updated. How effectively do you do this?

✓ Have a communication objective and plan for each point on your communication compass

Effective Team Characteristic 31:
Uses Critique not Criticism

We don't always agree or like decisions, behaviours, actions or statements. To be effective, a team needs to cultivate a culture and an environment that allows questions, concerns and challenges to be raised in a constructive manner.

A good example of raising a concern or challenge in an unconstructive manner is criticism. It is likely to cause offence, especially if it is personal and challenges personal values, behaviours and actions.   Criticism will often result in defensiveness and will impair the abilities of the parties involved to work through the issue constructively.   It is also likely to damage relationships.   Careful critique, which focuses on the impersonal, such as tasks and facts is likely to be more productive.

As a leader, ensure that the team agrees that criticism is undesirable and that they will take care to raise challenges constructively. The aim is to promote healthy debate – not for the sake of debate or 'point scoring' but to achieve the best result for the team.

Critique is a useful technique. It is not criticism. The technique can be learned and practised by the team and will lead to more constructive debate and analysis and hence better decisions.

The 3 Phases of Critique

The checklist below provides way of conducting a critique based on facts, balanced between negative and positive, supporting and opposing arguments.   This technique systematically challenges *statements, actions and behaviours* without engaging in outright criticism.   It therefore seeks to avoid disrespect or offence to the individual that could cause blocks in progress and participation, as people resort to fighting or fleeing from the criticism and or any associated conflict.

Phase 1: Analysis

What is the main purpose of the statement, action or behaviour?
To whom is the statement, action or behaviour directed?
What are the main points being made or demonstrated?
What are the arguments being put forward to support the statement, action or behaviour?
What is the observable evidence that supports taking issue with the statement, action or behaviour?
What are the underlying assumptions, beliefs and values supporting the statement, action or behaviour?

Phase 2: Evaluation

Is the argument presented logical?
Are the facts presented accurate?
Has the importance of the statement, action or behaviour been clearly articulated?
Are the arguments presented supportive of the main premise of the statement, action or behaviour?
Is the statement, action or behaviour appropriate for the audience that received it?
Are alternative and opposing views presented or ignored?
Does the argument presented help the listener and observer understand what is happening?
What emotional reaction is the statement, action or behaviour creating?
Is the emotional reaction strong or weak?

What particularly is it about the statement, action or behaviour that evokes the emotional reaction?
What is the root cause of this reaction?
When is the statement, action or behaviour taking place?
Is this an appropriate time for the statement, action or behaviour?
How does this statement compare to the views of others?
What is the statement, action or behaviour suggesting or implying?
What does this statement, action or behaviour make you think about?

Phase 3: Interpretation and response

On the whole, how do you interpret the statement, action or behaviour?
What do you interpret as the intent?
How do you interpret the objectives of the statement, action or behaviour?
What is your opinion of this statement, action or behaviour following analysis and evaluation?
Can you explain your argument and how you may agree or disagree with the facts or premise of the statement, action or behaviour?
What evidence and facts do you have to support your opinion?

Use positive reinforcement to embed the use of objective critique as opposed to criticism into the team's culture. As a team, take pride in your ability to challenge, question and debate effectively and the higher quality ideas, solutions and decisions that result.

Effectiveness Tips:

- ✓ Challenge in a constructive manner. Focus on achieving a better result for the team, not scoring points for yourself
- ✓ Make criticism alien to the team's culture
- ✓ Use the critique method of questioning to promote challenge that focuses on facts and driving better outcomes
- ✓ As a team, take pride in your ability to use healthy challenge and debate to deliver higher quality ideas, solutions, decisions and improve your performance

Effective Team Characteristic 32:
Knows who is influencing whom and when to act

As a leader, helping team members improve their influence will help their career, their confidence and their self-development. As team members grow and change they will influence you as a leader, other team members and different parts of the organisation in different ways.

Effective teams maintain an awareness of the changing influence landscape.

Leaders and teams who don't pay attention to, or understand the map of influence can be caught out by not knowing how information really flows. This could affect the perceptions of others outside the team of the leader, the team and performance. The impact of this on the leader and the team could be significant, particularly in highly political organisations.

Leaders and teams need to scan the influencing landscape and be alert to potential issues. In the worst case, team members are trying to influence others for their own benefit, not the team's. This could be someone who is pulling against the team or 'feathering his or her own nest'.

This behaviour ranges from subtly moving 'camp' and aligning with other teams, through to outright subversion. These behaviours are often characterised by a reluctance to share information, to report or allow others, even the leader into the individual's area or reporting more information to a colleague in another unit than to their line manager. This is of course selfish, destructive behaviour and has no place in an effective team or unit - but unfortunately it does happen on occasion.

Mapping the networks and influence of team members is a useful start to managing influence rather than letting it run its own course.

To map influence, use a technique such as a Relationships Diagram. Draw the individuals and use arrows to join them, showing the relationship between two individuals. Use arrowheads to show the direction of influence and the thickness of the arrow to show the strength of the relationship. In the case of two-way influence where one influences the other more, use differently sized arrowheads to show the degree of influence.

Use this technique to understand who is influencing whom, the strength of the influence and whether, in terms of achieving your objectives, it is positive or negative. Devise a strategy to reinforce and support positive influence and neutralise, combat or weaken negative influence.

Supporters and detractors

An effective team manages their stakeholders and delivers their needs. It also knows who its supporters and detractors are.

While in theory, meeting stakeholder needs will lead to stakeholder satisfaction, the reality is that some individuals and teams will actively support your performance and others will not. Individuals will have mentors and advocates; teams are the same. In the same way there will be detractors. These are people or units that do not support the performance of the team. For example, we have all heard the phrase 'those in the X office are ok but those in the Y office never get it right.' In other words, stakeholders can have very different perceptions of the performance of particular units even when their actual results, when measured objectively, are very similar.

Some organisations are very political or have many cliques. In some extreme cases, detractors can threaten the very existence of the team. An effective team is able to identify these groups and has consensus on their existence, position and needs.

Understand how your supporters can help you more (and how you can help them), engage them, work closely with them and work to turn them into advocates for you and for your team.

Leader Exercise: Know your supporters and detractors

Ask yourself who are the people, groups and teams that:

- are vocal and quiet supporters of your team and its performance in the organisation?

- are vocal or quiet detractors of your team and its performance in the organisation?

- who rely on your performance for their own success?

- need to perform so that you can succeed?

Assess how strong you think your relationship with each party is. How well do you know their needs and agendas?

Do your answers highlight any opportunities for you to increase your understanding, improve these relationships and your team's effectiveness?

Effectiveness Tips:

✓ Maintain awareness of the influence landscape

✓ Manage influence rather than let it run its own course

✓ Understand how information really flows and what implications this has for you as a leader and your team

✓ Be alert to any behaviours that undermine the team and negatively impact perceptions, performance, relationships and morale

✓ Know your supporters - help them to become advocates

✓ Know your detractors; understand their needs and their agenda. Build relationships and understanding where possible

Effective Team Characteristic 33:
Recognises contribution and results

Recognition is important for the motivation and development of the team and its individual members.

In your role as a leader, you need to make clear what you and the wider organisation regard as important and what you and the organisation will give recognition for.

As a leader, the recognition that you give must support and encourage the values and the culture (defined as 'the way we do things around here') of the organisation. This is providing that, the culture is not the very thing that you need to change for the organisation to be effective. If that is the case, the recognition you give should be aimed at driving the team towards the new culture.

Recognition is not the same as reward and its link to the formal salary and benefits processes. Recognition is part of how we demonstrate what is important to the culture and to the organisation. Some of the ways we do this are by the:

- signals we give
- rituals we perform
- stories we tell
- symbols we create and maintain
- structures we create
- processes and systems we create and perform in
- routines we maintain
- way power and influence is dispersed
- way innovation and ideas are fostered
- improvements we make
- engagement we encourage

- questions we ask
- interest we show
- time we spend
- rewards we deliver **and**

in the recognition we give.

Recognition is an effective way to involve, engage and motivate team members in developing the team's culture and aligning goals. It can also be a powerful way of contributing to an individual's growth. Positive reinforcement of what people do well, the award of a new promotion, career opportunity, or other form of self-actualisation are all strong forms of recognition. But, as we all know, you can never underestimate the power of just saying 'thank you.'

Recognition is positive reinforcement that creates momentum and makes people feel valued and appreciated. It promotes a strong sense of purpose and encourages further effort and improvement.

As a leader, if you focus recognition on improvement in attitudes, skills, knowledge, behaviours, processes, measures, customers and results, you will send clear signals as to what is important.

As recognition and positive reinforcement has such a significant impact on performance it is a fundamental tool for leaders to use when developing an effective team.

Both across a team as a whole and for each person individually, recognition can raise morale and develop increased self-esteem and self-worth. This will encourage the behaviours and outcomes you wish to develop and reinforce, as well as individual commitment to improvement.

Many companies have recognition schemes and these can provide a great opportunity for the leader to give recognition in a way that is open, understood and meaningful across the organisation. This helps with perceptions of fairness and equality.

Recognition is far more than what is in the 'recognition scheme' or the items in the 'recognition cupboard'. It is the fundamental way in which praise and motivation is given day to day, from little words of thanks and encouragement through to public acknowledgement, certificates, or gifts of tangible items or experiences.

Recognition and positive reinforcement has a vital part to play alongside critique and criticism in changing behaviours. Using critique helps focus on the facts of the issue and develops intelligent analysis, questioning and constructive challenge.

Criticism however, is the opposite of recognition. It can dilute the impact of any recognition given and counteract positive reinforcement.

Criticism affects morale and engagement, typified in comments heard 'around the water cooler' such as:

"I have been picked on again for trying to improve rather than they (the leader) picking on those who are not trying to improve and do nothing"

"My appraisal and one to one had lots of time spent on the mistakes I have made and all the good things got barely any attention, if mentioned at all."

"We spent all our time discussing the problems and no time developing on the good skills I have, to make them better".

"Praise seems always to go to the manager not to us on the ground".

As a leader, using recognition and reinforcement as part of developing a culture that values its people and delivers its goals, it is useful to remember:

What gets

- Measured
- Recognised
- Reinforced
- Rewarded

Gets done and improved

Whilst this phrase has been around for decades, it still holds true and can be related to by people in all different kinds of teams and industries. Remember this phrase and how using it helps maintain focus.

Recognition helps to create a supportive environment and a belief that people wish to give their best. Recognition however, must be given when behaviours support the goals and values and is deserved. Giving recognition that is imbalanced in its weight, such as large praise of one thing and small of another that seemed to have a greater impact, will create confusion as to what is important, or worse, give the impression of favouritism.

Recognition therefore needs to be balanced and most importantly be:

- Meaningful to the team
- Meaningful to the individual

Recognition can be financial, psychological or developmental but it must resonate with the individual concerned. It has to be personal. There are many examples where this isn't considered. For example, the team golf day where 10% hate golf or the team night out after a long effort away from home when in fact many of the team members just want to be given some free time back with their families. Recognition needs spontaneity (at times), considered timing and to be personal. To ensure that your recognition has the desired impact, take the time to consider the needs and recognition preferences of the recipient.

Timing is another critical consideration. It needs to be immediate or very close to the event so that it is relatively fresh in everyone's mind, improving both the impact of the recognition and its positive reinforcement.

Giving personalised, immediate and meaningful recognition can stimulate the individual and the team to improved performance and boost morale.

Remember as a leader that all the people will to some degree resonate with this very long standing sentiment:

"the greatest humiliation in life, is to work hard on something from which you expect great appreciation, and then fail to get it"
Edgar Watson Howe (1919)

Types of recognition

There are basically two types of recognition:
- Intrinsic - a demonstration of appreciation with little cost
- Extrinsic - some financial cost involved

There are many opportunities to give recognition, including:
- One to one verbal thanks

- Team meetings and briefings
- Walk the floor and talk to people
- Promote the achievement to the wider organisation
- Special recognition events
- Anniversaries
- Performance reviews
- Coaching sessions
- Letters, awards and certificates
- Key events marking the achievement of a goal or effort
- New career opportunities

In order to be effective, if the extrinsic approach is taken, it is vital that it is accompanied by intrinsic appreciation.

Manage your approach to giving recognition, observe the successes and failures that you achieve and learn from these. Do not just leave it to chance or side-line it because of other pressures.

Avoid:

- cheap, insincere and hasty recognition
- giving recognition because the process says so, as it comes across as false
- vague statements about who and what is being recognised and why
- an inconsistent approach to what is recognised
- disproportionate recognition

Remember, a person can remember a compliment all of their lives, and long after financial and other rewards are forgotten. When a person leaves a team or an organization, quite often the only things that they will take with them and keep are demonstrations of recognition, no matter how small.

Leaders Exercise: Assessing and improving recognition

Assess how effectively you use recognition:

- What kinds of recognition do you give? How often?

- When was the last time you gave recognition?

- What was the last kind of recognition you gave?

- Are you clear about what you give recognition for?

- How is your approach balanced between recognition, critique and criticism?

- What are the values and cultural aspects of performance you are trying to enhance and reinforce using recognition?

- Who receives recognition for what and is it balanced? You can use the checklist on the following page for some examples as a guide.

- Looking at the checklist on the next page, are these prompts important to you or do you have another list that is more important? If so, what does it include?

- How are you known in the team for giving recognition? What is your brand, style and reputation in this regard?

- How are you known in the rest of the organisation and to your leader in this regard?

- Do you know the recognition preferences of your team and each individual?

- What can you observe that tells you that your use of recognition is having the desired impact?

Recognition checklist:

meeting stakeholder requirements	community involvement	focus & commitment to meeting goals
handling complex issues effectively	delivering lasting results	leadership by example
sustainable success	customer service	coaching
role clarity	loyalty	teamwork
right first time	results	resourcefulness
managing risks	innovation	creativity
significant discretionary effort	continuous improvement	proactivity

Effectiveness Tips:

✓ Use recognition to positively reinforce the values and cultural behaviours that contribute to the team's culture and the delivery of its goals

✓ Tailor recognition to the preferences of the individual

✓ Give sincere, personal and honest recognition, make it personal to you and to the recipient not just part of a process

✓ Remember the impact of the public approach on the individual, the wider team and group

✓ Timing is critical

✓ Ensure that the reason, rationale and the measurement criteria for the recognition is clear

✓ Assess the mix of extrinsic and intrinsic recognition used. Always supplement extrinsic with sincere intrinsic personal recognition

7 Learning

The effective team has a strong focus on continuous improvement. It learns at the individual, team and process level and feeds this learning into continuous improvement.

Development plans are in place and actioned for each individual and for the team as a whole.

Individual as well as team development is prioritised. The effective team actively gathers feedback from stakeholders to improve the effectiveness of its outputs, and takes time as a team to share and learn from mistakes and experience.

The effective team is aware of how it reacts to issues and change and uses these experiences to continuously improve its performance.

Effective Team Characteristic 34:
Learns and continuously learns

A learning team is a team that has every chance of becoming an effective team.

One characteristic that typifies high performing teams whether they are sports teams, work teams or teams from other fields is their ability to learn.

Both the individuals and the team as an entity learn. Sometimes the learning is about facts and competencies, sometimes about people and relationships. Whatever it is, the team is on a continuous path of learning.

What is striking when you speak to or hear people at the top of their game is how often find a degree humility. You also discover that the most talented are often the people who turn up to training the most and practice the most. Even though they may be the 'best' they set even higher bars for themselves.

Some of the greatest athletes are acutely aware that others are trying harder and working longer and focusing more. This holds equally true in the competitive business world. This underlying self-motivation to excel and perform at even greater heights typifies a great team.

In the workplace we are faced with different motivations. People come to work for a variety of reasons. Some may not be motivated by the work they do but by the ends it achieves for them, while others may be motivated by the work itself. Some may wish to have a dynamic career and are focused on achieving that in the company they are with. Some may see the organisation as a stepping stone rather than an end. All of these different motivations affect the pace and depth of learning that a team can achieve.

How well each individual and the team learn from mistakes and opportunities will have a significant impact on how well the team performs and is able to improve its performance over time.

Examine how your team learns and look for examples that support your thoughts. If you think that your team can and should do more, put learning on the agenda for team meetings to reinforce its importance and highlight the need for action. When mistakes are made, or opportunities are not realised, make sure that you have a process for the team to discuss factually what happened and what they have learned. Document and implement any actions that will incorporate this learning into the team's continuous improvement processes.

Training & Development

Each team comprises a mix of personalities, skills, competencies, years of service, expertise and experience. The individuals will have a range of motivations and needs, including development needs.

Whilst the team must function and develop as an entity, team members need to feel that they are developing both within the team and individually.

Many companies have formal appraisal processes and they often include a Training and Development section. Unfortunately in many cases this is the most neglected and informally reviewed part of the appraisal. Discussions often happen annually or semi-annually and are sometimes linked to pay reviews so the focus is on results achieved. While this is appropriate, it is interesting how quickly the development section can be glossed over or treated as a 'box ticking' exercise.

An indication of poor leadership is when the team leader abdicates their responsibility to help you and the team move forward, leaving development entirely up to you. Leaders should see the development of the skills, capabilities and competencies of their people as a key part of their responsibilities.

Actively taking ownership of your own development and making it work for you is a positive step. Although you can take personal ownership, in most organisations you will need the support of your manager or leader. Whilst the leader cannot actually do the development or training for you, they can make a major contribution to your development through coaching and facilitating your growth. Coaching is covered in more detail in Section 8.

Again, leadership that cuts the individual adrift to manage his or her own development often typifies poor teams. It is interesting that many leaders are not judged by their peers or senior leaders by their ability to coach and develop their people. Perhaps this is because many in are leadership positions due to their technical competence rather than their ability to lead people. An effective team will prioritise coaching and development; its leader will exercise these competencies day to day not just at formal review time.

Leader Exercise: Prioritising staff development

- Does everyone in your team have a formal development plan?

- Is it only discussed at full and half year reviews? Or is progress against this plan formally reviewed at regular one to one meetings through the year?

- Do the development plans include actions for you as the leader as well as for the team member?

- Is the completion of the actions rigorously followed up?

One way of ensuring that this process actually happens is to put it in it your formal objectives and ensure that your direct reports do the same for their people. Making this commitment reinforces the importance of development in your team culture and links its delivery to the formal assessment of *your* overall performance.

How does your own leader prioritise your development? What steps can you take to improve this so that you, as well as your people can continue to develop?

Career and lifelong learning

Teams have a transient life. It may be that the team itself stays intact for some time but the membership changes. Each time a new person joins or leaves the team, a new team is formed.

Look at your organisation over a certain time period and list all of the structural and people changes – you might be surprised at how many there have been. Think about yourself and the teams that you have been a permanent or temporary member of over the last few years. Whatever those teams were and whatever the organisational structures they appeared in, you have been developing your career through them. They will have exposed you to, and taught you many things.

Progression through teams is an integral part of career development. In many senior roles it is the ability to run and lead senior teams that is critically important. In many circumstances, the team and particularly project teams are used as a formal way of exposing people to new and broader thinking. They also expose individuals to new techniques and other functional areas of the business that they may not be familiar with.

An effective team uses individuals in various teams and sub-teams to help develop them and their career. Personal development can be accelerated by the overt recognition that the teams you are in today are actually learning opportunities.

An important characteristic of an effective team is that it is aware of this career development aspect of the team and openly discusses how issues and opportunities that face the team can be used to enhance careers and support individual development.

Team Member Exercise: Identify career learning and development opportunities

- List the learning opportunities currently presented to you within your team

- List the wider learning opportunities that present themselves or could be developed, for example, in the organisation, outside the team or outside the organisation

- Plan actions for seizing these career development opportunities

---

Effectiveness Tips:

✓ In order to be an effective team, you have to be a learning team

✓ Ensure that each individual and the team have development plans

✓ Regularly monitor progress and actions against these plans

✓ Ensure that the team has a strong process to gather feedback on its outputs and that this feedback is used to continually refine performance. Review the effectiveness of these changes

✓ Take time as a team to learn from shared experiences, from expertise and from mistakes

Effectiveness Characteristic 35:
Understands their strengths and weakness

An effective team is aware of strengths and weaknesses, both of the team itself and across its value chain. It is able to openly review them and work together to improve performance.

A SWOT analysis ⌞_⌟ is a useful technique to assess strengths and weaknesses.

SWOT stands for:

- Strengths
- Weaknesses
- Opportunities
- Threats

Conducting a detailed SWOT can reveal issues, which then enables the team to develop action plans to capitalise on strengths, grasp opportunities and address weaknesses and threats. The SWOT will also help the team recognise what it is good at and what is it not so good at to raise awareness and improve cooperation and support amongst the team members.

Review the SWOT a couple of times a year to keep it fresh or when the team membership changes. Ensure that the team maintains a common view of the results and keeps plans for change and development up to date.

Another benefit of the SWOT is that it can help keep things objective within a team and help keep the focus on tasks and depersonalise issues. This can help take the emotion away from challenges particularly when the team is under stress.

Being aware of the team's opportunities and threats helps the team maintain focus, supporting efforts to realise opportunities and take action to address threats.

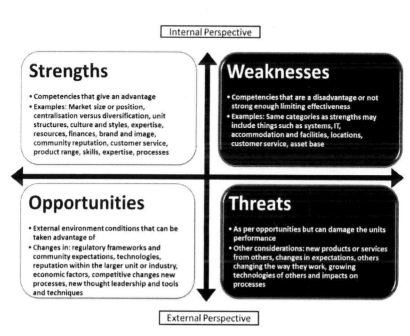

Internal Perspective

Strengths

- Competencies that give an advantage
- Examples: Market size or position, centralisation versus diversification, unit structures, culture and styles, expertise, resources, finances, brand and image, community reputation, customer service, product range, skills, expertise, processes

Weaknesses

- Competencies that are a disadvantage or not strong enough limiting effectiveness
- Examples: Same categories as strengths may include things such as systems, IT, accommodation and facilities, locations, customer service, asset base

Opportunities

- External environment conditions that can be taken advantage of
- Changes in: regulatory frameworks and community expectations, technologies, reputation within the larger unit or industry, economic factors, competitive changes new processes, new thought leadership and tools and techniques

Threats

- As per opportunities but can damage the units performance
- Other considerations: new products or services from others, changes in expectations, others changing the way they work, growing technologies of others and impacts on processes

External Perspective

Figure 14 SWOT: Strengths, Weaknesses, Opportunities and Threats

Effectiveness Tips:

✓ Use a SWOT analysis to understand your strengths, weaknesses, opportunities and threats

✓ Use action plans to capitalise on opportunities and strengths and address weaknesses and threats

✓ Keep your SWOT analysis up to date and refresh when circumstances change

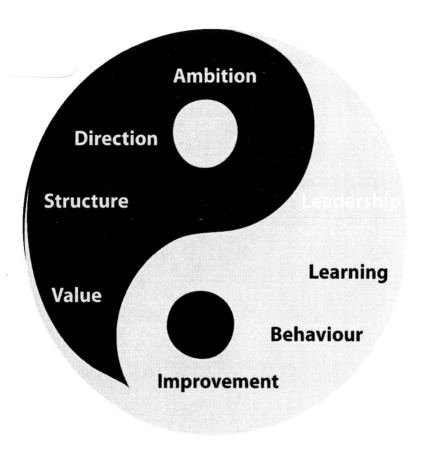

8 Leadership

The leader of the effective team varies leadership style and develops leadership at all levels, with a strong emphasis on coaching to support Team Effectiveness and personal and team growth.

The leader of the effective team ensures that the team remains agile in times of change in order to respond to the organisation's changing priorities, while staying focused on long term goals.

The team has strong leadership and robust governance and management control processes.

Effective Team Characteristic 36:
Uses coaching as a powerful leadership style

In a situational leadership approach, there are various styles a leader will deploy based on the situation, the competence and experience of the team and its members. These include directing, coaching, supporting and delegating. One leadership style that often does not get the right amount of attention is coaching.

Know when you are coaching

Coaching is an important leadership style and part of the leadership activities of the effective line manager.

To some, coaching means getting a specialist coach. Whilst this is a useful step for many, it doesn't take away the need for the line manager to coach. Unfortunately many people in leadership roles do not see coaching as part of their job, possibly because it is time consuming and requires special skills to coach effectively.

As a leader, it is important to know when you are coaching and when you are managing. There are times when you will need to be directive and at other times a coaching approach may be needed in order to facilitate development.

It is also important for your people to understand when they are being coached so that they can participate effectively in the coaching experience.

To contrast managing and coaching: as a manager, you will set goals for a team member with them and review progress towards achieving those goals throughout the year. As a coach, you will:

- look at the way the process of setting and reviewing goals works for both of you

- discuss how these objectives fit with other needs, and
- discuss ways the individual can adjust their approach, behaviour and acquire skills in order to achieve the goals.

In this way, a coach will be helping the individual learn and develop as an integral part of the process of achieving their goals.

In another example, the leader will define the team's vision and it is up to the team members to relate to it. When coaching, the focus will be on working with individuals to help them understand how their behaviour and performance is contributing to the vision and helping them develop in these areas so that they can contribute more effectively.

Make sure that you are clear on the separate coaching needs of the team and of each individual within it. Have coaching needs specifically defined in the team's development plans.

Coaching is not the sole province of the leader. In effective teams, team members will actively coach each other to develop individuals and take the team forward.

Coaching is also too often confused with a 'let's change to coaching now' syndrome. Coaching, although often positioned as a special event to give it some structure, is best used integrated with day-to-day activities.

Coaching is also often confused with simply getting a person to do a task more effectively. Whilst this is partially true, it vastly underestimates the impact and scope of coaching. Coaching has a simultaneous emphasis on continuous development, improvement, learning and relationships as well as task performance and goal alignment. That is why coaching can be very powerful.

Coaching styles vary considerably depending on the situation, how complex the development activities are, the capabilities, skills and competencies of the individual and their attitudes, values and beliefs.

Coaching is about helping a person achieve their potential and grow to achieve success at a higher level. Coaches provide the frameworks, compass, road maps, blueprints and stimuli to help people move along a journey, discover their potential, the resources they need and widen their capability and horizons.

Some say that the origin of the use of the word coaching goes back to the idea of an old coach that would transport a person along. In many ways this carriage, which helps a person move, is the essence of coaching. One thing is clear - a coach is helping a person on a journey of self-discovery. It involves movement and travel. It seeks personal insight and requires self-awareness from the individual concerned to recognise the need to learn and make use of the coach.

Coaching requires clear goals so the journey can commence and an understanding of where you are now so that the direction of travel can be set. Coaching also involves trial and error, pilots and experiments. Without these excursions, tests and trials no learning takes place and it will be unclear whether progress is being made towards the goals.

Coaching is a complex task in itself. Do not underestimate its depth. It requires a range of approaches, such as posing questions for the coachee to reflect on and try to discover the right answer for themselves, role modelling, demonstration or discussion and description.

Coaching Approaches

According to Wageman and Hackman[23], there are basically five approaches to coaching depending on ability and motivation. These approaches range from the directive to the nondirective.

'Tell' Approach - Operant Conditioning

The most directive approach is where the coach tells the team how to behave then monitors behaviour and gives recognition and reinforcement based on their original instructions. This is suitable in some circumstances particularly in low competence or early team stages. It does not always secure the behaviours desired, particularly over time. If you see a coach or manager that 'tells' all the time, bear in mind that this approach is unlikely to result in change over the long term. When used for team coaching, it has limited effectiveness, as it does not take into account the varied levels of competence and maturity of the team members.

Coach Led Approach – Eclectic

This approach is where an external coach is used, who has tools, techniques and practical processes that help the team progress. If the external coach demonstrates expertise that the line manager does not have, team members may start to gravitate away from their line manager towards the coach for day to day help, direction and coaching. This coaching style is more directive as the knowledge and skills lie and can remain with the coach.

Behavioural Observation and Feedback Approach

This approach is where the coach observes the team at work and their behaviours. The coach then feeds that back and takes the team through an analysis and conclusions.

The discussion then moves on to how to improve from what has been observed, discussed and concluded. This is helpful as a journey for the team but the coach retains the expertise used in the process.

Process Approach

In this approach the coach helps the team move through two aspects of performance. Firstly, analysis of the business processes around a particular issue and what happens in that process and secondly, around team member interactions. The team takes charge of analysing what is happening and draws out the lessons for improvement.

The multi-method approach

This approach to coaching a team consciously, and that is the operative word, uses different coaching approaches at different times in the team's lifecycle. The coaching is long term and is not done on a 'fly-in fly-out' basis.

As a leader, manager, coach or a person that is in a team being coached, be very clear on why the coaching is taking place, the kind of approaches that can be used and the desired outcomes.

Do not underestimate the value of coaching versus other leadership and team development approaches. Choose to coach consciously rather than unconsciously and approach it with the same rigour as all other leadership activities.

Effective Team Characteristic 37:
Is agile and focused

Across the organisation some of us are part of many forums, groups and teams, in addition to our own team. As a leader, a part of ensuring effective team performance is recognising and managing your and your team's involvement in a changing mix of temporary and permanent working groups and the impact this has on your own team and performance.

Project teams form and have defined life spans. Organisational units may also have a 'life-span' but that is often less clear and regarded by most as more stable. However, when most of us consider how many reorganisations we have actually been part of, permanent work teams or organisational units may not look as stable as we like to think.

At the beginning of the year, a team agrees its goals and plans its activities and the resources it needs to achieve them. At this point, the team may generally feel very clear on what it needs to do and how it will work towards achieving this.

As the year goes on, new opportunities and business issues emerge that were never foreseen during the initial planning and resourcing phase. In response, new initiatives and projects are researched, and launched, all requiring resources. Some of these initiatives might be resourced and implemented within your team. Some might be organisation wide projects that demand a representative from your function to provide technical expertise or participate in governance or just to be a part of the overall effort. Sometimes you might find out about a project second hand, which may impact your functional area or your ways of working depending on how it is implemented. In this case, you might voluntarily send a representative from your team to ensure that any changes proposed include your views, needs and input.

As a consequence, you can soon find that large numbers of your team are spending significant amounts of their time out in the wider organisation contributing to these projects. You will often find that it tends to be the same people, time and time again. Your best, most experienced people.

Obviously this means that they are spending substantial amounts of time not contributing to the team and not delivering the team's agreed goals and objectives. Your resources are helping to deliver someone else's objectives. This may negatively impact the wellbeing, morale and effectiveness of your team. These external initiatives and projects will probably be short term in nature - your team is here for the (relatively) long term and exists to deliver for its customers.

However, this is the reality of working in large organisations today. As a leader, what can you realistically do about it?

If you do not measure the extent of this problem, you will not be able to quantify its impact and will not be able to take action.

The first step is to identify all of these activities. Ask each person in your team to list out all initiatives and projects that they are working on that are not part of the team's agreed goals and objectives. This should include how much time they are spending on each and the likely duration of the activity.

Using this information, see if and where you need to act:

- challenge all activity to see whether it is absolutely necessary that your team provide resources to it

- assess the impact of this extra work on the morale and wellbeing of your people, and

- assess whether you now have the right structure and resources to deliver your goals and objectives. If not, consider restructuring, asking for more resources, or negotiating the dropping or the delay of some of your deliverables.

Use the data you have gathered to keep your stakeholders informed of the issue, any potential impact it may have on your delivery to them and to support any negotiations on resourcing and overall delivery.

If your people are taking on significant amounts of extra work, don't forget to monitor their wellbeing. Take action to recognise their efforts, keep them motivated and see them rewarded appropriately.

Effectiveness Tips:

✓ Maintain a strong awareness in the team of team goals and deliverables

✓ Be aware of the extent that your team members are working on other needs of the organisation. Document this if it becomes significant and use this to discuss the impact of this additional workload on your delivery and resource needs

✓ If team members are taking on significant amounts of extra work for the organisation that cannot be avoided, provide recognition and support and monitor their wellbeing

Effective Team Characteristic 38:
Management as well as leadership

There is quite rightly a strong focus on leadership when we discuss effective teams.

However, an effective team is built on a strong foundation of robust management as well as leadership.

It is easy to become so preoccupied with the vision, the building of the future and directing change that some of the more structural frameworks, routine tasks and controls slip.

Styles of leadership such as delegating, coaching, supporting and directing are all vital components of building effective teams. Equally vital are: planning and budgeting activities, structuring and organising the team, allocating responsibilities and accountabilities, risk management and controlling the day to day and planned developments.

Effective teams have strong leadership supported by strong management.

Leader Exercise: Management and control

Identify your primary management activities and check the balance between your leadership and management focus.

- List, in priority order, the primary management processes you must complete each year

- Place these onto a high level timeline or Gantt chart

- Use this high level chart to discuss and plan with the team the primary management processes that must be completed during the year

- Add any others from the team's perspective

- Use this as a live document throughout the year to keep all primary management cycles and processes in view and to allow adequate planning and time for completion

- Use this document to review the year and to plan next year's activities, incorporating all of the learnings of this year into your scheduling and resource planning

9 Conclusion

Teams are the core building blocks of a today's organisation.

Teams are a key mechanism for the achievement of goals and objectives.

Team Effectiveness:

- *Is critical in today's organisations*

- *Requires definition and the understanding of its DNA in order to be lead, managed, developed and improved effectively*

Leaders:

- *Benefit from a construct that allows them to keep the key dimensions of Team Effectiveness in view*

- *Benefit from practical guidance on how to improve the effectiveness of the key characteristics of the dimensions of Team Effectiveness*

Team Effectiveness: Putting it all together and measuring overall performance

An effective team is defined as one that:

1. Satisfies its agreed stakeholder and value chain requirements first time, every time - at lowest cost and with minimum variation

2. Engages everyone in teamwork, and continuously learns, develops, grows and improves the individual, processes and the team itself to achieve its potential and its goals

3. Has agreed goals, strategies, structure, processes, behaviours, stakeholder support and leadership that enable the consistent and improving performance in the above

4. Manages change in an agile, flexible, effective and efficient manner with balanced respect for the needs of the organisation, team and individual.

The Team Effectiveness Model provides a construct for understanding and improving Team Effectiveness. It groups 38 key characteristics of effective teams into 8 Dimensions to provide focus to improvement activities.

As a first step towards improving your team's effectiveness, it is useful to:

- Analyse your current performance across the 8 Dimensions
- Assess the team's strengths, weaknesses and identify development opportunities
- Create an action plan for change and development, and

- Develop a Team Charter to capture critical statements, intents, commitments and underlying principles in one place to facilitate focus, communication and action planning.

Like the principles espoused in this book what gets measured gets done. To support you on your effectiveness journey, there are two key tools available for you to download at **www.iwise2.com**:

- a **Team Effectiveness Model Assessment Tool**^{TM} (TEMAT^{TM}) that you can use with your team to assess your current effectiveness and identify development opportunities.

- a **Team Charter to capture** the basis of what your team is all about and the results of the assessment process to provide a solid base for the team's interactions, relationships, goals and action planning.

Use the framework of tools and techniques presented, the Team Effectiveness Model Assessment Tool^{TM} and the Team Charter as your roadmap for building, leading and sustaining an effective team.

Notes and further reading

1. Rubin, I. M., Plovnick, M. S. & Fry, R. E. (1977) 'Task Oriented Team Development' New York: McGraw-Hill

2. Maslow, A. H. (1954) 'Motivation and Personality' New York: Harper & Row

3. Katzenbach, J. & Smith, D.K. (1993) 'The Wisdom of Teams: Creating the High-Performance Organisation', McKinsey & Company

4. LaFasto, F. & Larson, C. (2001) 'When Teams Work Best: 6000 Team Members and Leaders Tell What It Takes To Succeed'. Thousand Oaks, CA: Sage

5. Hackman, J. R. (2002) 'Leading Teams: Setting the Stage for Great Performances', Boston: Harvard Business School Press

6. Schwarz, R. M. (1994) 'The Skilled Facilitator: Practical Wisdom for Developing Effective Groups', San Francisco: Jossey-Bass

7. Lencioni, P. (2002) 'The Five Dysfunctions of a Team: A Leadership Fable'. San Francisco: Jossey-Bass

8. Cohen, S. G., Ledford, G. E., & Speitzer, G. M. (1996) 'A Predictive Model of Self-Managing Work Team Effectiveness' Human Relations, 49 (5), pp643-676

9. Tannenbaum, S. I., Salas, E., & Cannon-Bowers, J.A. (1996) 'Promoting Team Effectiveness' In M.A. West (ed), 'Handbook of Work Group Psychology pp503 - 529, West Sussex, England: John Wiley & Sons Ltd

10. Ratcliff, R., S.M. Beckstead and S.H. Hanke (1999) 'The Use and Management of Teams: A How-To Guide', Quality Progress, June

11. Adair, J.E., (2009) 'Not Bosses But Leaders: How to Lead the Way to Success', 3rd Edition, Kohan Page, London and Philadelphia

12. Tuckman, Bruce W., & Jensen, Mary Ann C. (1977) 'Stages of Small Group Development Revisited', *Group and Organizational Studies*, 2, pp419 - 427.

13. Kaplan, R. S. & Norton, D. P. (1996) 'The Balanced Scorecard: Translating strategy into Action' Boston, Massachusetts: Harvard Business School Press

14. Covey, S.R., Merrill, A. R. & Merrill, R. R., (1999) 'First Things First: Coping with the Ever-Increasing Demands of the Workplace', UK: Simon & Schuster

15. Belbin, R. M. (2010) 'Team Roles at Work' 2nd Edition, Oxford, UK: Butterworth-Heinemann & www.Belbin.com

16. Thomas, M.M, (2011), IMAGIINE^{TM}, www.iwise2.com

17. Tannenbaum, R. & Schmidt, W. H. 'How to Choose a Leadership Pattern', Harvard Business Review, May-June, 1973, pp162-175

18. Covey, S.R., (2004) 'The 8th Habit, from Effectiveness to Greatness' UK: Simon & Schuster

19. Schindler, P. L. & Thomas, C. C. (1993) 'The Structure of Interpersonal Trust in the Workplace', Psychological Reports, 73, pp563-574.

20. Scott, C. and Jaff, D. (1989), 'Managing Organisational Change', California, Crisp Publications, p26

21. Jung, C. G. (1968) 'Analytical Psychology: Its Theory and Practice', Routledge and Kegan Paul, USA

22. Myers Briggs. I. revised by Kirby, L.K. and Myers, K.D. (2000) 'Introduction to Type: A Guide to Understanding Your Results on the Myers-Briggs Indicator', 6th Edition, European English Edition, OPP Limited

23. Hackman, J. R. & Wageman, R. (2005) 'A Theory of Team Coaching', Academy of Management Review 30(2): 269-87

Further reading

Blanchard, K. (2010) 'Leading At A Higher Level', UK: Pearson Education Limited

Vermeulen, F. (2010) 'Business Exposed: The Naked Truth About What Really Goes On In the World Of Business' Great Britain: Pearson Education Limited

Anderson, M. (2010) 'The Leadership Book' Great Britain: Pearson Education Limited

Hackman, J. R. (1987) 'The Design of Work Teams', in J.W. Lorsch (ed.) Handbook of Organisational Behaviour, Prentice Hall, Upper Saddle River, NJ

Bergman, T. J. & De Meause, K. P. (1996) 'Diagnosing Whether an Organisation is Truly Ready to Empower Work Teams: A Case Study', Human Resources Planning, 19(1), 38-47

Further reading continued

Wellins, R. S., Byham, W. C., Wilson, J. M. (1991) 'Empowered Teams: Creating Self-Directed Work Groups that Improve Quality, Productivity and Participation', Jossey-Bass, San Francisco

Belbin, R. M. (1997) 'Changing the Way We Work', Butterworth Heinemann, Oxford, UK

Kinlaw, D. C. (1991) 'Developing Superior Work Teams: Building Quality and the Competitive Edge', Lexington Books & University Associates Inc, San Diego, California

McLean, R. & McNicol, A. (2010) 'Team Work: Forging Links Between Honesty, Accountability and Success', Penguin Group, Victoria, Australia

Zenger, J. H., Musselwhite, Ed., Hurson, K., Perrin, C. (1994) 'Leading Teams: Mastering the New Role', Business One Irwin, Homewood, Illinois, USA

Jacobi, J. (1965) 'The Psychology of C. G. Jung', (1965) 7th Edition, Routledge and Kegan Paul, USA

Adair, J.E. (2010) 'Leadership and Motivation: The Fifty Rules and the Eight Key Principles of Motivating Others', Koran Yale, London

Published by

First Published in 2011 by

iWise2eBusiness Limited
57 - 59 High Street
Dunblane
Scotland
United Kingdom
FK15 0EE

www.iwise2.com